AFTER COLLEGE:
THE BUSINESS
OF GETTING
JOBS

AFTER
COLLEGE:
THE BUSINESS
OF GETTING
JOBS

JACK FALVEY

 **WILLIAMSON PUBLISHING**
CHARLOTTE, VERMONT 05445

Library of Congress Cataloging-in-Publication Data

Falvey, Jack, 1938—
    After college.

    Bibliography: p.
    Includes index.
    1. Job hunting—United States. 2. College graduates
—Employment—United States. I. Title.
HF5382.75.U6F35   1985   650.1'4   85-22640
ISBN 0-913589-17-9
Cover and interior design: Trezzo-Braren Studio
Typography: Villanti & Sons, Printers, Inc.
Printing: Capital City Press

Williamson Publishing Co.
Charlotte, Vermont 05445

Manufactured in the United States of America

10 9 8 7 6 5 4

C O N T E N T S

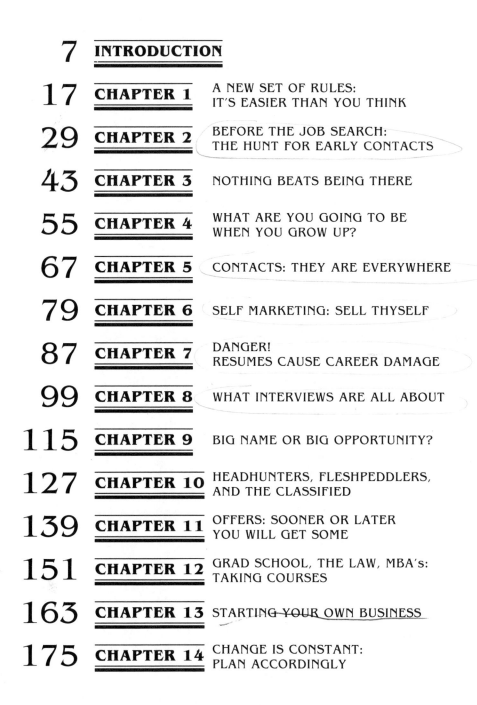

DEDICATION

To Ed McMillan, professor at Bunker Hill Community College, Charlestown, Massachusetts, whose outstanding example of everyday work with students caused the writing of this book. And to Tom O'Loughlin who feels that undergraduates are people, too, and who convinced me that part-time teaching is worth the effort.

ACKNOWLEDGEMENTS

I have read many acknowledgements in countless books and now have a chance to write my first one. Even a small book, such as this, requires the efforts of many people. Jack Williamson liked the idea and became father to the child as all publishers should. Susan Williamson translated the manuscript into English from the thought groups I like to write in. Her editing was a major effort. Phyllis Read decoded my handwriting, no small feat, and typed and retyped every word you will read. Special thanks to Ellen Kolton who suggested that I write in the career field.

Howard Smith of The Paper Mate Division of Gillette, provided the refills for my pen (it took one-and-a-half). Ed Wohlmuth, an experienced author, explained the rationale of each step in the arcane process of creation and publishing. My class at University of Massachusetts at Boston tested titles and lent student perspectives. The manuscript was read and commented upon by: Mrs. G.H. Falvey (mother) who thought every word was wonderful, V.J. Pappas and Russ Bleemer of *National Business Employment Weekly*, Bob Hennessey, Barbara Jones, Mrs. David Huestis, and Mary M. Falvey, my wife, who proofread each step and lived with me during the entire process described above. (Many have said this last act was the most difficult of all.)

THE TRANSITION: COLLEGE TO THE WORLD OF WORK

L ate in the spring each year, feature writers for newspapers and magazines do articles about the "job market" for graduating seniors. They write about this or that major being in high demand, and they quote starting salaries that, for some reason, never seem to be available to real applicants. Almost always in these articles are a few horror stories about English majors driving taxicabs or chemical engineers working in gas stations. No doubt the examples are true, but they are not caused by some external market factor, as is so often implied. They are caused by the lack of knowledge, understanding, and skill of the graduates in being able to market themselves in the real world of jobs and work.

> **Getting a job is not an isolated event that happens every now and then. It is much more like a continuum.**

What a great waste of the investment made in a college education and in the lost potential of the graduates who lack the one final ingredient in their education—how to make a proper, profitable exit.

After College: The Business of Getting Jobs assures that you will never appear in one of those articles as a sad and sorry example. For the most part, life after college—and it's a good one—is very different from how students generally perceive it. Once you understand the differences, and you will by the time you finish reading this book, you can begin doing the things that pay off in results, rather than spinning your wheels chasing nonexistent leads.

Getting a job is not an isolated event that happens every now and then. It is much more like a continuum.

It's a whole series of ongoing events that comes together at different times, providing opportunities and challenges.

Look at what it took to get into college. It wasn't just a question of taking SATs, filling out forms, and sending in the cash. It may have involved an interview during which all of your communication and presentation skills were used. It could be that your ability in sports, developed over many years, played a part in getting you into the college world. It may have gone back many more years to a parent's college choice, making you the offspring of an alumnus, and, therefore, in a special selection category. So many factors contribute; you never can be sure which one (or ones) will become the deciding factor.

The same is true in getting jobs. All kinds of pieces fit together. Some come together in unexpected ways. You can't plan everything, but you can be aware of what works both for and against you. When something fits, run with it. The world of work has a completely different set of priorities from the ones you are now living with.

Open your sensibilities to what's important on the "outside" and put aside some of the old priorities of college. Take, for example, "The Cume." In a few months, it will never be mentioned or thought of again. You will not be numerically ranked according to some semiarbitrary point system for the rest of your life. The slate will be clean. Your background will be general, not specific. You will become an entry-level employee, a member of a team. You will not be a "something" major with a 2.6 average. You may never be asked for a transcript of grades again. Life without "the cume" is a good one.

> **You will not be a "something" major with a 2.6 average. You may never be asked for a transcript of grades again. Life without "the cume" is a good one.**

Before you begin your academic retirement party, however, keep in the back of your mind that at a future date you may want to flirt with some kind of graduate school. In that case, academic numerical respectability may be of at least limited value.

Life, on occasion, takes some strange turns. One academically inept undergraduate managed to complete four years with a C- as his highest grade in any course. Not what you would call an academic all-American. Because of some career successes later in his life, he was asked to guest lecture at a number of universities. As a result of those lectures, one college wanted him to become a part-time member of its evening school faculty. It fit with his schedule and he thought it would be worth doing, so he began teaching at the college level in his specialty with good results. As an administrative formality after three months of teaching, he was asked to send along a transcript of his college grades from twenty-years past. He did. They went in the files with no one even looking at them. Whew! In this case a bona fide academic horror-show was dug up after twenty years, and it had no effect even in the college world of credentials and degrees.

The world is full of superstars with below-average academic records.

Although grades are a big thing right now, they will become a minor point and cease to have importance in only a short time. If they happen to be great, wonderful. Take a great deal of pride in the talent and self-discipline that produced them. But, even high grades unfortunately have a diminishing value curve. If they happen to be marginal, don't worry. The world is full of superstars with below-average academic records.

A second example of the shifting sands of values is course selection. You probably have put a great deal of effort into selecting the perfect mix. Again, this will have limited and diminishing impact in a short period of time.

Micro Computers 404 may look like the ticket to technology; in fact, a technology company may not care about your experience with what may be, in their race car world, just a horse-and-buggy exposure. The fact that both vehicles move on roads is interesting, but has little other than conversational value.

Colleges are not very good at vocational training. Being concerned about course mix and a tight cluster of related subjects may seem important and logical to you now, but, once again, you will see that although these efforts won't do any harm, they won't be of great value either. What will be of value is building skills in many areas untouched in college. Interview and social skills, which are highly valued in the working world, just don't appear automatically when you need them.

GET YOURSELF READY—NOW

Sort of have the feeling that this is going to be some transition? Right. But don't worry because thousands and thousands of people have made it without difficulty. Radical changes in emphasis and values are just a fact of life. What they change to will be of great interest. You will be using and developing different skills. Studying by yourself in the library and taking pencil and paper tests is obviously not where the future is. Count your blessings.

The values in the world of work are much more socially oriented than academically or technically oriented. Conversational skills, appearances, and interestingly enough a good general education will play a big and expanding role in the future. Being "well read," for example, will show, and pay dividends. You may have many of these skills already. If so, all you need to do is keep moving in the same direction.

You may not be at the top of your social game or be as outgoing and articulate as you would like. Make some moves in those directions. Can you believe that going to a few parties may be a good way to improve in this area? Focusing on areas for improvement will start you moving in the right direction.

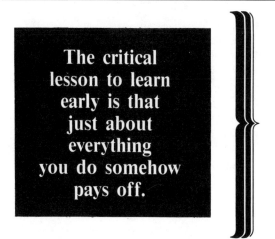

The critical
lesson to learn
early is that
just about
everything
you do somehow
pays off.

Lead time is part of the new game. One factor of never-ending fascination is how we prepare and work to get ready for one eventuality, only to find at some later date, all of our carefully planned work sets us up for a completely different result. The critical lesson to learn early is that just about everything you do somehow pays off. This is a good reason for setting high personal standards. Often it pays off in different ways than anticipated, but it always seems to somehow fit. Jobs, careers, life-planning—call it what you will—happen to be far more art than science. Knowing all kinds of approaches, and understanding how pieces and people can be made to fit together are great creative challenges. Understanding that it is not a science and that no reliable formulas exist will make you much more comfortable as you progress through the maze of building what you will ultimately look back on and call your career.

But, then, you are already pretty good at mazes. Take a look at what you have done so far. You have met the challenge. You have measured up. You have made it through college without too much difficulty. The next steps are no more difficult than the last few. In some cases, they will be many times easier, more creative, and satisfying.

The options unfolding, and the means to get where you are going, are almost infinite. That's good news because it means there are so many different directions available, it's almost impossible to pick a wrong one. But, if you should, it becomes a simple matter to just shift a little, and move on out in another direction. Being fast on your career feet is another skill we will discuss.

Think of the student who selected a major in industrial management. By taking courses in methods' analysis, purchasing, personnel administration, factory layout, and all kinds of similar and related subjects, a job in industrial engineering seemed to be the logical first step after graduation. After interviewing with a number of big companies and taking all of their mechanical aptitude tests, the fact slowly dawned that most of the other applicants for these jobs had mechanical engineering backgrounds. Needless to say, the offers were slow in coming, and when a few finally were made, they were not very good.

In the interest of going to work, our overprepared (but in the wrong direction) student finally took a job in sales, as a way of earning a living until a vocational light would dawn on the horizon. The background in manufacturing came up again and again in his career, as it gave him the ability to communicate with engineers and company presidents alike. It was never wasted for a minute; it just was put to a completely different use. A surprise? Yes. Did it all fall together neatly? No. But it did come together, and it became part of a career mosaic, a subtle pattern which is played out in the overall picture. It's hard to go wrong because even the strangest pieces can be made to fit somewhere, sometime.

Not having all the required skills can sometimes be turned into an accidental benefit. Again, there are no "right" courses in these instances. A junior manager was asked to produce a training film for a trade group. He relied heavily on an outside audiovisual house for help. By working with a talented writer and director, the manager acquired some very advanced skills without ever going through the basics. As it turned out, the basics were easy to pick up in reverse order, and in a short time he began doing industrial films on his own, by using a skilled team that filled in his technical deficiencies completely. Without any background in film or theater arts, he became a moderately skilled, successful writer/producer of generic video material, which eventually was used by thousands of companies around the world.

If you are beginning to see a pattern, you'll recognize that it is more of a mosaic, a career mosaic. Once you finish college, what you do no longer will follow a linear progression. Junior year will no longer come after sophomore year. Sophomore year may extend for two years, if you do not understand the system or happen to take a few inopportune turns. On the other hand, things often move at an accelerated pace and in strange directions.

> **Once you finish college, what you do no longer will follow a linear progression.**

Step-by-step time blocks, although they do exist in some career moves, can often be disregarded. The rules are very, very flexible. You have to push them in order to get them to move, but they are movable. Going from college to the outside is a move from structure and time-based steps to flexibility and action-based elements.

Now is the time to start. Some college students say that what they are looking for in their first job is a training program to give them a chance to build the new required skills. What they are really saying is that they want a continuation of the world they are already in. They are comfortable by this time with instructors and courses and curriculum management. A nice two-year training program seems to be ideal. Although these programs do exist, they tend to postpone the time when the business of doing a job must be tackled.

Self-directed learning never ends, or should never end, no matter what you do. The sooner you come to grips with the concept that you must seek an opportunity to contribute and participate, the better. Along with real

> **Going from college to the outside is a move from structure and time-based steps to flexibility and action-based elements.**

work comes a very steep learning curve. That's part of the action. What also comes with a real job is the satisfaction of actually doing something, and being held accountable for your actions.

A dramatic illustration of this concept was the experience of a new graduate from King's Point Maritime Academy. A third officer's license in the Merchant Marine comes with the degree. Landing his first sea-going job on a tanker had him on the Atlantic, standing watches, on his second day at work. Unlike a Navy ship where all kinds of officers are on and off the bridge at all hours of the day and night, on a tanker, the watch officer is often the only officer.

A few days later, under normal rotation, our man drew the midnight watch which also happened to coincide with the ship's approach to the Straits of Gibralter. There he was on the bridge of a huge tanker about to go through one of the most heavily traveled seaways in the world. The weather was good and the ship made it without incident, although in recounting the story, it seems that the stretch marks of personal growth for our now experienced officer were considerable. He still can't believe the captain never even woke up.

Relax! Life after college is not that difficult. Different? Yes! Challenging? Yes! Fun? Can be. Think about it. No more buying and selling of almost useless, unreadable textbooks. No more sitting through endless, almost meaningless lectures. No more institutional food, and long lines for everything. No more convoluted schedules of 8:00 A.M. and 9:00 P.M. classes with nothing in between. No more being kept up half the night because of someone's stereo mania. No more lotteries for housing. No more exams. No more tight money crunches (well, hopefully).

Get ready to be welcomed into the world of getting it your way. Of being able to concentrate on one thing at a time and learning what you must know in short order. Of being able to meet and associate with superstars or at least highly competent contributors. Of being able to travel, live, eat, and dress like a successful person (even though you won't have much money for a while). Of being asked for your opinion almost from day one, whether it seems to count or not. Of seeing what you do matter in a real, if small, way.

Get ready for what amounts to a very exciting treasure hunt. It will have its ups and downs for many years to come, but it is about to begin. Let's see how the pieces are starting to fit together in your life, and what your first moves or next moves might be.

The time frames are open and flexible. You can begin working on some of the techniques as early as the end of sophomore year. Even two or three years out of college, you can step back, re-evaluate career directions, and begin again. All without penalty because somewhere, somehow those first mosaic pieces which seemed to be wasted or off in the wrong direction will come back to fit into a future part of your career.

What an adventure! On to some of the new rules of this new world you will soon be visiting, living in, and sailing through.

A NEW SET OF RULES: IT'S EASIER THAN YOU THINK

**Keep in mind
all you need is
one job. It's not
necessary to
mount a product
marketing
campaign
throughout
American industry.**

L et's take a look at how this new game works.
Keep in mind all you need is one job. It's not
necessary to mount a product marketing
campaign throughout American industry.
Although it may be the biggest thing on your horizon,
what you are trying to do is no big deal. Thousands of
people are hired every business day. Once you see how
the process operates, you will begin to see how to fit
yourself into the flow.

There is an ever-moving pipeline of people. Coming
out of one end are retiring company presidents,
department heads, staff people, those who have been
fired, employees of companies that have gone under,
have been acquired, or are discontinuing a division,
people who have decided to move to another industry or
part of the country, or whatever. There is a flow of
people. On the other end of the pipeline, there is a never-
ending need for input. In good times and in bad, for
better or for worse, in every area of the country, to
greater or lesser degrees, there must be people coming in
to fill the pipeline. If organizations are to continue to
operate, there must be constant input of people.

There are at least fifteen million companies in the
United States. They are located in almost exact
proportion to population, so it isn't difficult to figure out
where they are. They are where the people are. The bigger

the crowd of people, the more companies in the area. There is just about an unlimited amount of entry-level opportunity in just about any location you can choose. This doesn't mean that a job is easy to come by, but if you know there are jobs out there, and you know roughly where they are, getting one becomes a much more directed task.

One last macro point to consider. Entry-level jobs requiring the least amount of experience are the most abundant and are obviously the easiest to get. Looking at it from the other side of the desk, bringing in bright, usually young, green but enthusiastic new people is a low-risk, inexpensive investment. Entry-level employees come in at the bottom of the pay scale. They can be given work that no one else wants to do. They have no bad habits and can be trained to do things properly and efficiently. They are idealistic because, perhaps, they don't know any better. They are coming from an unreal world (academia) and can be molded any way the organization chooses. What better deal could there be for an organization?

Your point of view? You are a great bargain for any company that offers you a job. They can't get along without new people, and you are the lowest-cost, highest-potential new person they could imagine. You have much more to offer than you may think. Keeping this in mind is important, because it will make your approach far more positive and effective.

All this is not fiction. In *The Soul Of A New Machine* by Tracy Kidder, the strategy developed by Data General to catch up with the competition in building a new 32-bit computer was to go out and hire engineers directly out of college. Why? Because these green employees wouldn't realize what was to be asked of them was just about impossible in the stipulated time-frames. No one already in the company or in the industry at large would commit to the kind of work that was necessary to meet the deadlines and get the product to market.

Data General put together its team, and proceeded to burn it up. The project was successful, the engineers involved eventually recovered, and, in retrospect, didn't get a bad deal. They were able to get several years of entry-level experience in several months' time. They even had the added benefit of being written up in a Pulitzer

Prize-winning book. Of course, you really don't want to get involved in that kind of a deal if you can help it, but it illustrates that what you bring to the party is of great value. You can be absolutely assured there are many people out there looking for someone just like you.

If there are large numbers of entry-level jobs in every area of the country that must be filled by low-cost inexperienced applicants, you can conclude that tapping into this system shouldn't be as difficult as you might have guessed. You are correct with a big IF—if you understand the big picture. When it comes down to specifics, sometimes getting the job you want is difficult.

If you can keep what you are trying to accomplish in perspective, you will be much looser and, therefore, better able to complete your task.

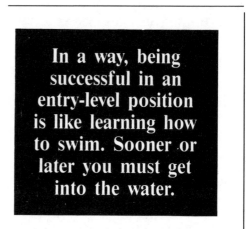

In a way, being successful in an entry-level position is like learning how to swim. Sooner or later you must get into the water.

JUMP IN!

In a way, being successful in an entry-level position is like learning how to swim. Sooner or later you must get into the water. You can learn to swim at the Olympic Training Center at Mission Viejo in Southern California with an East German professional coach, or you can do your first strokes in a local "Y" pool, a country lake, or any ocean that you can get to. The essential ingredient is water. The objective is to be able to move through the water unsupported. It can be learned anywhere. Big body of water or small, the rules of physics apply with equal force.

The Fortune 500 holds an unwarranted mystique for the entry-level person. Having a name to drop when

Two-year training programs in reality are jobs that keep you from doing anything meaningful for a couple of years.

asked where you will be working is of considerable ego value. Don't think for one minute that these companies don't recognize their name value and trade heavily upon it with extended entry-level assignments. They also sell two-year training programs which in reality are jobs that keep you from doing anything meaningful for a couple of years. They restrict you from earning other than proscribed wages for that period and often for a much longer "dues paying" segment of your career. The programs are often just two-year interviews. Ugh!

Following those big name training program career tracks can be OK, provided you understand that you are on a railroad that goes in one direction only; someone else controls the stops, speed, ticket prices, and where and when you get off.

You may say at this point that your big worry is getting on, not off, and who cares about all the rules of the game. You can deal with those later. True, but a few hints up front will add perspective to what you are trying to do and that, in turn, should influence your entry strategy and tactics.

You can continue to work the progression strategy if you like. The right prep school leads to the right college, leads to the right company, in the right industry, with the right assignment, in the right division, and so on ad nauseam.

Business can be much more fun and lead to a fuller career and life, if you will just be a little more open and flexible in your thinking. A progression strategy still can be built, but it should fit with what you discover you like, rather than following what appears to be "the way."

Big company or little, this industry or that, this location or that city doesn't make a great deal of difference just so long as you get started, because from

Mobility and maneuver are some of the names of the new game you will be playing.

It is like picking a point from which to jump into the ocean; there is more than one best place to make an entry splash.

here on in you set the schedule. Mobility and maneuver are some of the names of the new game you will be playing.

Knowing that there is a big wide world of opportunity out there is one thing, getting into it is another. It is like picking a point from which to jump into the ocean; there is more than one best place to make an entry splash. You must pick one place and one time, so sooner or later getting down to cases is essential.

Let's start with the time. D Day (departure day) shouldn't be difficult to plot. There is always the option of being a professional student and staying on forever, but let's not get into that because it has all kinds of different rules that apply in no other world. What we want to work on are the strategies, principles, guidelines, and even old wives' tales of the "outside world." So start with the date you will enter the outside world and then work backwards to today to determine your lead time. If you can spread the process out over eighteen months, that's great. If you have already passed the mid-point of your junior year, it just means you have to pack a little more into a shorter time. Anywhere from six to ten months will do, but if you are down to zero months, well, there is no time like the present. Jump in. One rule that will become apparent very quickly is "things take longer than they do."

> **People are not add-ons to the system; they are the system.**

THE PEOPLE FACTOR

The single common denominator in all business and organizations is people. Everything comes down to people, trust, friendship, and the building of these kinds of bonds. Some will last only a few days or weeks; others will last a lifetime. You have been in the people world all of your life, so it isn't a foreign place. It's just that from here on in the intensity of relationships starts to build. Your task is to cultivate and nourish those relationships that will enable you to do the things you choose to do. Relationships take time to build, and they endure best when not rushed. Beginning now, your job is to start to make contacts.

People are not add-ons to the system; they are the system. For better or for worse, that's what you have to work with. "Who you know" is said with disdain only by those people who don't know anyone. Denying the social facts of life is just as silly as denying the biological facts of life. Dealing with relationships, building new ones, developing old ones, and leaving behind those that should be left behind is a never-ending process to be nurtured all along the way.

When you approach IBM, or Exxon, or Ding Dong Technologies, you will not be dealing with the legal corporate entity. You will be dealing with one key person. Identifying that key person and testing the waters to see if a relationship can be built are the underlying tasks that face everyone, at every level. At entry level, the situation is no different. The challenge of human relations is the most important challenge of all. Focus on that critical element.

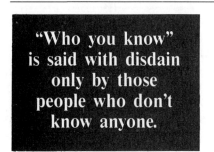

> "Who you know" is said with disdain only by those people who don't know anyone.

> **Technology changes, organizational structures change, whole industries come and go, but the single factor that stays is the people factor.**

If you can build relationships, everything else will follow. Sometimes you only need to build one in your whole lifetime, if you build the right one, but the usual case is that you will build many relationships of varying degrees of depth, length, and value.

In the normal course of things, you may develop hundreds or even thousands of relationships. It doesn't make much difference; the methods apply across the board. Entry-level positions, as well as all future positions, depend upon specific people and your ability to get to know them and they you. For openers, you can begin to see why the resume, cover letter, and the screening interview system leave something to be desired in building unique, meaningful, and productive relationships.

It is said that we are in a service business economy and there is no better way to deliver service than with warm human contact. Begin to think in terms of human elements no matter how structured the form and formalities of the system seem to be.

SHARPEN YOUR COMMUNICATIONS SKILLS

College life does not foster those skills that are most useful in getting the outside world to sit up and take notice of you. You have had to sit without talking for long hours, taking notes while lectures drone on. You have had to study in silence in a library or whatever quiet place you could discover for yourself, and you have had to take exams in solitary states of zero communication. Even with all those formal systems against you, there are ways and opportunities to begin the process of building the people skills and contacts from which the fabric of the outside world is made, while still in college.

You don't have to become a campus activist. Begin to look, however, at the opportunities you have to make contacts. Meet people, find out about them, see what their circle of friends and relations are all about, and generally work the crowd.

What do you want to know about the people you meet? Who are they? Where do they come from? Where are they coming from? Where are they going? What do they bring to the party? Most people won't come up to you with a printed biographical sketch. You have to discipline yourself to develop an interest in the contact process, and begin to ask the questions that will open up relationships. You want to give out minimal information about yourself, while finding out as much about others as you can. There is no mystery to it. The rules of conversation dictate that the more you talk, the less time available for incoming communication, so begin to test the techniques of asking questions and listening to the data that result. Watch interviews on television and observe how to draw people out. Watch the follow-up questions at news conferences or even the give-and-take techniques of the late night couch-and-desk programs. Then try them out.

See how much you can find out about someone without being offensive. Try it out on friends or their friends. See if you can get some time with someone senior to you, and get comfortable with the game at that level. You don't have to turn yourself into an extrovert. It's possible to be an excellent communicator, even if you are shy and a little put off by the whole business.

A classic example of these skills can be seen in the film *Being There.* If it is available to view, by all means spend the time to see how relationships are developed with minimal language and social skills. The plot revolves around a character who has little brain power, but has learned a few key phrases in order to get through life. He just uses them over and over in every situation he encounters. He merely says that he "understands" or that, "You look good today." He mentions people's names and he listens intently even though he actually understands little. Not that you want to emulate this virtual emptiness; it's the process in the film you want to see. With a few key questions and an understanding of the techniques, you can become an adequate conversationalist. Interestingly, if you talk to a group at a party, asking all kinds of questions while saying little about yourself, you will find that the group is left with a very high opinion of you.

Asking good questions is a key skill area to work on. You can begin anytime. Applying it for the first time in job acquisition situations is not the best way to produce results. Getting your skills put together first is the method of choice. The world after college is very, very broad and the skills necessary to make moves in that area should be built well in advance.

OPEN YOUR EYES TO OPPORTUNITY

By understanding that the world of work is much more fluid and less structured than anticipated, that it is not as time-based as you might have thought (although parts of it can be), and that people skills are most important, you begin to get a sense of the task at hand.

The mechanics of the process are important, but one of the biggest and best surprises is to discover that the system often operates without formal mechanics.

One student was asked to do a class project that involved going out in the field with a professional in a subject-related discipline. She set up the meeting and spent the day as assigned.

In the process of the day's work, she met the field advisor's boss. When she called to say thank-you a few days later (she had already sent a written note), the person told her that his boss would like to chat about her impressions. A week later she and the boss had lunch and a nice informal discussion. She said that the day in the field was just what was needed for her course work, but that it was also very exciting by itself. The job looked challenging, and it seemed to be fun as well. Two days later she had a call back from the boss asking if she would be interested in joining the company upon graduation.

There was no application, no cover letter, no interview. She just made a good impression. She was judged to be bright, ambitious, energetic, and a perceptive person (not a superstar). On the basis of those impressions, she was offered an entry-level job. She couldn't believe that this was how the system worked. The person who hired her was on the lookout for talent. Because the relationship was less than formal, a relaxed rapport developed easily and the boss was able to get an excellent initial impression. The person she worked with in the field chipped in a positive opinion, and the offer was made.

> # The woods are full of opportunities.

> ## The unconventional is much more common than you may think.

> ## Consider for a moment that over 98 percent of companies in the United States are family-owned and that includes some 35 percent of the Fortune 500. Think of all the people in those organizations who are qualified by genes alone.

Take it any way it comes. The woods are full of opportunities. Becoming sensitized to them and making appropriate responses is not difficult to learn. The unconventional is much more common than you may think. The more you see it, the more you understand it, the better player you will become when you choose to play.

Structured qualifications are not the only entry-level elements that count. Consider for a moment that over 98 percent of companies in the United States are family-owned and that includes some 35 percent of the Fortune 500. Think of all the people in those organizations who are qualified by genes alone. If all those relatives can make it, regardless of ability, there is certainly room for you.

Not only is there room, but corporations can't get along without you. With just reasonable attention to people skills, you can qualify for some incredible opportunities. Ability, talent, and all the extras you have to offer are bonuses.

You are about to get involved in a venture that has few rules that can't be bent or broken. Almost anything goes; it's just a question of figuring out what fits when and where and how. The criteria are very subjective and often can't be anticipated or prepared for.

All this is good because the same factor that eliminates you from one opportunity will be the element that most impresses the key person in the next encounter. Now you can begin to see why the formulas and rules don't always work, and why some people just seem to luck out. It's the underlying principles that are important, because they give you the awareness to identify potential and to adjust to situations.

The complexity of the challenge and potential reward involved will increase as a career progresses. In its simplest form, it's just a case of making friends. Not much more and not much less. Let's see how best to do it.

CHAPTER 2

BEFORE THE JOB SEARCH: THE HUNT FOR

CONTACTS

Organizations are just big clubs. The process of getting a job is one of attempting to join one of these clubs.

When you are outside the system trying to look in, it is difficult to see how things actually work. It's really quite straightforward and not that complicated. Organizations are just big clubs. Different people have different duties that require different skills and sometimes different personalities. Accountants are of a certain type, research people fit into a particular mold, sales types are just that, and so on through just about every function. Each of these groups works across disciplines with other groups, but most of the time is spent with junior and senior members of one's own group.

The process of getting a job is one of attempting to join one of these clubs. It is a social, personality, background-type match that you will be trying to make. In the trade, it is called good chemistry or gut feel. When you work with someone, you are in close contact with that person over an extended period of time and, therefore, if at all possible there should be a minimum of friction and as much compatability as possible.

BEWARE OF PERSONNEL DEPARTMENTS

When junior managers are taught to interview, they are told to try to suppress their initial impressions long enough to accrue enough information about an applicant to see what depth exists. Few managers—few people—can do this. We all make judgements on superficial first impressions. Some people then proceed from that point and seek data to support the position they have taken.

What all this means is that first impressions, no matter how unfair it may seem, are important. They work two ways. First, they are very subjective. Life is subjective. No need to try and change that; it's just a fact you must work with. Secondly, by being aware of those things that make good first impressions (firm handshakes, neat dress, a friendly smile), you can be sure they are part of your opening approach to people. You may cringe at the superficiality of it all, but that's the reality. Work within it.

Stay away from the personnel department of companies (unless you want to work in one). The subjective opinions and judgements of personnel people usually can do you little good if positive, and considerable harm if negative. If most of what you can expect is negative, then seeking another route with greater chances of a positive outcome surely has merit.

Being screened out by the doorman without ever getting to meet the membership committee or club officers is not an experience your ego should willingly seek out.

Being screened out by the doorman without ever getting to meet the membership committee or club officers is not an experience your ego should willingly seek out. Having a member of the club escort you past the doorman without the doorman's inspection of your credentials is ideal.

That's not to say that organizations don't need personnel departments. It's just that one of their functions should not be the negative screening of talent, not at a professional level at any rate. If, as a manager, you needed fifty clerical or production workers in the next ten days, you would be delighted to turn that task over to personnel, and well you should. But personnel or "human resources" likes the idea of being able to project itself upward in organizations, so it often takes on professional screening functions. That's a bad deal for all concerned. In some organizations, personnel actually does the hiring, and the resultant hodgepodge and mismatches are less than productive for the individuals involved, as well as the corporations.

Keep uppermost in your mind that you are trying to join a club. It may be a sales club, it may be a manufacturing club, it may be a finance club, or it may be a small general club where many members do many things.

Whether the club is in the world's biggest corporation or a one-person shop, someone somewhere has to say yes to you. One person must sponsor you. If the sponsor can make the decision himself, great, but if he needs higher authority or approval, then he must decide that you are the one he wants, and that he will sell your case to get approval to bring you on board. That is a bigger yes, but still it's one person you have to convince. If he likes you and wants you as a new member, he will do what must be done to get you in. If he doesn't like you for any reason, there isn't much you can do about it, so look for another sponsor in another club.

It's that subjective and that simple. On the other hand, if you don't like the organization, the sooner you decide that it will be a poor match the better. Don't block out your own feelings about the people you are meeting just for the sake of joining an organization and getting a job.

The person you will be directly reporting to will become one of the most important people in your life. Before you sell yourself body and soul, you should know as much about that person as you can.

CONTACTS ARE EVERYTHING

How is all this done? Where do the contacts come from? How do you get to meet key people? How do you find your way into this other world without using personnel departments? How do you keep from becoming a recruitment statistic? How do you keep your resume out of the big pile? (Not sending it in is a good start.)

The treasure hunt, the club membership, the job all begin with a contact. A person. If you go straight to someone for membership in a club, you naturally will be told how exclusive it is, how difficult it is to get in, and, without knowing you very well, how to make the standard application.

The straightforward approach just doesn't work well in our society. It's just like meeting someone of the opposite sex. It's a social dance. You are introduced or meet at an open gathering. You make and receive a first impression. You trade a little information. If things are of interest, you decide to meet again.

Although there is such a thing as love at first sight, usually relationships take a while to develop. People are reluctant to make big commitments to one another without taking time to get to know the other person. Some, of course, will leap into a commitment. Yet, most of us have learned to be careful of fast, easy relationships. They tend to be less than lasting and often cause one party or another some damage or grief.

It seems that the slow and easy approach is best in the social aspects of life, and this includes finding a job. If you're feeling desperate to make the right contact, you just have to learn to cool it, so you don't scare everyone away. Good things take time.

In college, if you want to meet people, you join organizations, you get involved in projects together, you ask friends to introduce you, you seek positions of visibility, you ask senior people for information or advice, and, above all, you become active in the areas where the people you want to meet can be found.

If you want to pick huckleberries, you have to go where the huckleberries are.

The same strategy applies in seeking your fortune in the outside world of organizational clubs. If you want to pick huckleberries, you have to go where the huckleberries are. Or, if you want to know about what firemen do and you want to meet some, try going to the firehouse.

Now we all know of or have heard about the formal or structured system for doing this kind of thing. We sign up for on-campus interviews, we dazzle them with our resume and we get invited to visit the home office on the Coast.

If you happen to be Princess or Prince Charming, things can work that way. If you have enough going for you to make it through that screen, just think of what you could do with a free-form approach.

Most of us don't like the idea of being put through the ringer or being worked over by the system, but students who have lived in a regulated world for three or fours years usually can't resist following "the system" in the area of seeking jobs. Nothing wrong with signing up, but a quick look at the numbers will show that there are options with much higher returns open to almost everyone.

Only a tiny fraction of companies do any campus recruiting, so why limit yourself to just that little group. Why join a herd of twenty other people trying to make a big impression in a fifteen-minute interview? Do you have any idea what it is like for recruiters going to a college campus, sitting in a room for six or eight hours with a new smiling face in front of them every fifteen minutes?

The highlight of the day, believe it or not, is the no-show who lets them get a breath of fresh air.

> **The highlight of the day, for recruiters going to a college campus, believe it or not, is the no-show who lets them get a breath of fresh air.**

One technique campus recruiters use to keep applicants separated in their minds is to draw little stick figures on the forms. This creates at least a visual cue as to who might be whom, when they sort through the resultant mound of paperwork a day's interviews generate.

A little trick of the trade for applicants who want to play in this marginal league is to print their basic data on the back of an eight-by-ten photo of themselves. These are called head shots, and actors and actresses use them all the time. When you are selling a body, you might as well be remembered.

Guidance counselors will tell you that head shots are not professional. Provided they are well done and work, you can take that chance. Even if everyone used them (and they don't and won't), you would still be remembered—at least for what you look like.

THE INFORMATIONAL INTERVIEW

Back to the real business of getting to meet the members of the club. Students have a privileged position in our society. They are allowed to spend considerable amounts of time in the pursuit of knowledge. It's an accepted temporary position in life, and almost everyone has been through it; it is considered honorable. Most people can identify with the life-style and environment.

Students are like stray dogs. If they are friendly, people will take time to stop and pet them. Students also are supposed to do research and, therefore, the pursuit of knowledge through research is generally accepted as legitimate student behavior. If at the same time, one happens to make a potential job contact or two, what harm can come of that? And so, a hidden value to being a student begins to surface.

The so-called informational interview has now found its place in the organizational world thanks to Dick Bolle's *What Color Is Your Parachute* (Ten Speed Press). The informational interview is often abused by career changers, causing some high-visibility people in name companies to limit their participation in this practice because of the time involved. Students fortunately maneuver outside this insider's practice, and have a privileged status just by being students.

> **It is easier to meet directly with some vaunted vice-president than it is to work your way through the personnel interview tangle up to even a regional manager.**

It is easier to meet directly with some vaunted vice-president than it is to work your way through the personnel interview tangle up to even a regional manager. You may find it hard to believe that some senior management types would clear their calendars for an hour or two just to talk to a student, but they do it all the time.

You won't believe the number of ready, willing, and able big wheels out there just waiting for your letter and call. There are, of course, many vice-presidents who won't see you, but that's their loss. Besides, you don't want to work for an organization whose vice-presidents are working so hard, they don't have time to be human beings.

A letter, by the way, requires some kind of letterhead and stationery. Here is the place to spend a little cash. Make the investment in some high-quality paper stock and an attractive, professionally typeset letterhead. Resumes aren't worth the cost of the ink, but letterhead stationery is a high-priority, high-return investment. This may be the first visual contact you will make with a person, so making anything other than a first class impression isn't very smart.

Think in terms of monarch size (7-by-10½-inch paper) versus standard 8½-by-11-inch paper. The smaller size is acceptable, and you don't want to write long letters.

> **The less you say in your letter the better. You want a meeting, not a lifelong relationship.**

The less you say in your letter the better. You want a meeting, not a lifelong relationship. One step at a time. Here's how you might approach your first letter.

"I need your help. I am researching *blank* industry (profession). If I could meet with someone of your experience, I am sure I could get enough information in a half hour to give me the direction I need to begin finding out how *blank* really works."

"As a junior studying *blank*, it is very difficult to understand how everything applies or fits together."

"I will call your office to see if we can schedule a meeting."

Now don't copy this text verbatim but look at the technique of getting right to the point and not sending out all kinds of useless data.

The follow-up phone call is even easier, because often you don't even talk directly to your V.I.P. You can talk to a secretary or administrative assistant who handles the calendar. You simply call and say that you had written to set up a meeting and how does the calendar look? What are the best dates and times?

This easy little two-step will get you face to face with almost anyone. It just isn't that complicated. All you have to do is pick a few target people. Once you get to see one, then one of the objectives of the meeting should be to get a list of recommended people to meet next. Then you are off and running in the contact referral business.

GETTING STARTED

The first name can come from anywhere. What do your roommates' parents do for a living? Who was quoted in some article or news story? Is there anyone in the index in your textbooks who looks interesting? Did you meet someone last summer who works in a field that might be worth exploring? It's completely free-form. You can dig out officers' names from the back of annual reports, if you are desperate. You might just hit one. No need to chase after the president or chairman of the board. A nice comfortable V.P. will do just fine. Alumni directories are full of names. Some college career offices even maintain alumni contact files.

What about getting there? Nothing wrong with working over the local crowd for awhile. You don't have to start by running all around. If a trip or two is necessary, that's part of the hunt. Stringing a few meetings together is even more professional. "I have a two o'clock that day with G.E." isn't a bad line, if you want to see someone else in the morning.

Don't be too selective when you begin, because you don't have much to base your selectivity on in the first place. Go and see what is happening. How do you know international monetary management is where it's at? It may be, but until you have met with a half-dozen international moneterists, you can't talk with much authority.

Big ones, small ones, near and far, go take a look. Remember, even though you are going to look them over, they will be looking you over as well.

The little thank-you note you send out must be perfect and prompt. Get it typed by someone who knows how. It doesn't have to look like you did it yourself. Typing something out on a portable typewriter or a low-grade word processor printer may say that you can type on one of those machines, but is that the message you want to send?

Even though you are setting up, or attempting to set up, casual meetings, the consequences could be anything but casual, so keep the low-key information exchange as an objective, but treat the meeting as a higher priority event.

You don't have to look exactly like a miniature junior executive when you meet someone, but appearances are very, very important. Remember those subjective but important first impressions. Take the extra time to get a reasonably professional look to your outfit.

If you have questions in the area of appearance, make a few field visits to see what people have on. You are trying to join a club, remember, and you know members are most comfortable with people who look like themselves. Sort of basic, but these little things are important. Rather than reading a book on appearances, which may or may not be relevant to your specific needs, just begin looking around to see how these kinds of things are done. Look at the pictures in appropriate trade journals. Watch a business or industry program on television. See what people are comfortable with and then plan accordingly.

Once you actually get face to face with your target person, there is no need to knock him dead with your knowledge and personality.

Once you actually get face to face with your target person, there is no need to knock him dead with your knowledge and personality. All you have to do is get the person to talk about the things he knows most about, and you are home free. What's even easier is that it is an open book exchange. You are permitted and encouraged to work up a written set of questions in advance, and then actually read them off as you go along. What could be simpler? No studying, no unexpected questions, just the ones you planned in advance. You can even take some notes as you go along, so you don't have to remember everything that was said.

Remember that you are the interviewer in an informational interview. Being interviewed by someone who regards you as the authority is a pleasurable experience. If you do it even reasonably well, you will make a generally good impression.

So, again the double mission. Develop data, but do it in such a way that you make a good impression. You are there to glean information, not to land a job. Mixing these two objectives will short circuit the whole process. If you have the insulation of student status, this can be done easily. In fact, the earlier you begin, the better. Even sophomores can get in on this type of approach, but junior year is optimum.

Now that you have your questions answered, your notes taken, and a list of other "experts" to attempt to see, all you have to do is send a nice warm thank-you note mentioning some specific data that was of particular value or interest. See if you can show some analytical talent at this point by picking out some key elements to note in your follow-up.

> **You are there to glean information, not to land a job. Mixing these two objectives will short circuit the whole process.**

Just a line or two is all that's needed. Keep it short and to the point.

If, after going over your material and impressions, you think the chemistry was particularly good, you might want to do a meeting summary as a further follow-up. This can be promised in the thank-you note by saying that you would like to send along your detailed impressions in a few days to see how they fit with the real industry situation. This allows you to write a report for your contact. You don't want to do this for everyone, but if the iron is hot, why not press it a little.

What you are doing overall is showing, rather than telling people what you are all about.

Keep in mind that organizations run on social an communications skills. By demonstrating that you can make a polite professional contact, can question for information and then listen for detail, are courteous

> **What you are doing overall is showing, rather than telling people what you are all about.**

enough to say thank-you promptly (24 hours) in writing, and finally, if you choose, can demonstrate analysis and writing talents, you will have gone a long way in transition from student to professional status.

If all this sounds somewhat overwhelming and beyond what you think you can do, don't let it worry you, because it doesn't have to be done all at once nor does it have to be done perfectly the first time. The method can be practiced one step at a time; you may not go the whole nine yards on the first few tries.

Because the process is repetitive, you can do it over and over again, getting better at it each time and building countless contacts along the way. Of course, time is a factor, but it would not be difficult to do five or six informational interviews with two full follow-ups during the week of spring break. You might have to spend most of February and March setting up the week, but why not? No one is going to let you walk in without some effort. The effort part is what is seldom seen when looking at results. The effort in informational interviewing is considerable. The results can be impressive as well, so why not pick a couple of target people and work on them. All of your practice and effort will go towards building skills that are in general use throughout almost every career. It's time well spent no matter how you look at it.

MAKE IT A GROUP EFFORT

If you can get a student group together which will commit to a skill-building project as well as serve as a support group, you can all work together reviewing each other's efforts and providing encouragement when the schedule gets crazy. All this plus a course load? You bet. That's a good reason for the group effort because, on your own, much of this type of activity is easy to put off under the pressure of immediate academic needs. Because of the lead time required, getting started with contacts and informational interviews should be reclassified to "immediate needs." It's a good time to discard your linear view of the world and begin building a mosaic which seems a lot like juggling in the beginning, but will eventually start to hang together with more and more pieces dropping into place.

Without a priority, it's easy to think in terms of signing up for that old campus recruiter schedule when second semester senior year rolls around, and becoming a collector of all those "nice to have met you, but" letters.

Each career move you make will require that you do an inordinate amount of advance groundwork if you expect to achieve substantial results. This first career move is no exception.

Your first career move is an object lesson in the ongoing process. Get going. Stationery, target list, early contact schedules, support group, everything; it pays to be out in front on this one. The returns are incredible.

CHAPTER 3

NOTHING BEATS BEING THERE

Finding out what is going on by meeting key people is good; actually working with them for a period of time is even better.

⟩⟩

Finding out what is going on by meeting key people is good; actually working with them for a period of time is even better.

Without much attention or fanfare, so-called work-study programs have been going on for many, many years. The plan was to attend classes for a term or two, and then alternate between work and the campus in order to generate experience plus cash to support the academic life-style. It was originally an acceptable way to work your way through college before all the financial aid programs came into being.

A side benefit was that relationships, which often resulted in full-time jobs and careers upon graduation, were built during work-study assignments. Just as often students discovered jobs they would never want to do full time, and companies they would never want to join no matter what. The exposure to reality, while a student, provided a firm data base of both positive and negative impressions on which to build career plans.

INTERNSHIPS: AN INSIDER'S VIEW

Recognizing that the distance between the campus and the business world is often measured in light years, the logic of getting out there and looking around in advance of having to make a permanent move is not hard to follow. The questions are when, how, and with whom?

Enter the internship. Some industries or professions have recognized the benefit of exchanging inside professional experience for cheap labor for years. The master apprentice system has been in operation for centuries and, in some crafts, is still going strong.

Internships are just now beginning to be made available to students almost everywhere in almost every discipline. Broadcast and communications companies have large intern staffs. Some programs are formal; others are just one-person creations for specific persons and purposes, or for short periods of time.

But internships are there. Getting them is like a mini-job hunt. High visibility internships are more competitive (some may be created upon request), but the truth is there isn't a manager or professional who couldn't benefit from an intern, so the concept is valid across the board. If you can't find or fit into a formal internship program, it's well within a student's abilities to work on creating something in an area of interest.

One hard-pressed technical support manager in a consumer goods marketing department found himself working long hours on important but routine, time-consuming projects. He had no budget for temporary help and his company would not add additional people for his operation. A couple of college contacts and suddenly his department had all the staff it could use at no cost.

After the program was in operation for a while, he talked his company into paying token expenses for the students. What counted was that the students were getting a first class education on how a name company operated. They were meeting key executives as well as all kinds of outside vendors who came through the area where they worked. They were encouraged to get to know as many people as possible, so they could begin building their own contact network. As an added bonus, they

> **A flavor develops that's just about impossible to gather during informational meetings. Being there is what's required.**

acquired the name of the corporation to drop whenever they discussed their backgrounds and experiences.

Some colleges have short three-or-four day shadow intern programs that operate during spring break for juniors. Those students who are smart enough to give up Fort Lauderdale can visit and work with alumni in their jobs for this brief period. It doesn't sound like much, but it is amazing how much you can pick up in just a few days. A flavor develops that's just about impossible to gather during informational meetings. Being there is what's required. By all means, place internships high on

> **Although a job, any job, may look like a reasonable goal when you are on the outside looking in, be selective from the start.**

your priority list. Whether for a few days or for a complete semester or summer, they are very, very important.

A summer internship is good at anytime, but the end of junior year seems to be about the best time to get your act together, and set up a summer experience that will provide a window to the outside world.

The internship approach is an accepted strategy, carrying many benefits, not the least of which is the realization that a job is a two-way transaction. You can look over prospective employers during an internship and they can look you over as well. If things look good all around, the step-one internship often leads to a step-two job offer.

Although a job, any job, may look like a reasonable goal when you are on the outside looking in, be selective from the start. Take the time to carefully evaluate organizational climate and opportunities, for this is a big part of your transition strategy. It's almost impossible to know what goes on in an organization until you get inside. You won't know what people are like to work for and with until you actually do it.

You can test the environment in many ways, but the internship system is hard to beat for finding out if you fit with them, and of even greater importance, if they fit with you. This short-term relationship works well because both parties have an easy out. Meanwhile you can discover if there is opportunity in a particular field even if this particular organization doesn't suit you. You can meet some people and rate them on whether or not they are good to work with. Can you learn from them? Do you want to learn from them?

Where are the internships? Everywhere. One college freshman approached a guest panelist from a local television channel and ended up doing graphic arts support for the station for six weeks. She then parlayed this arrangement into independent study for course credit. She discovered that television was not the place for her. She eliminated one career option early on, while learning a lot about contacts and the work world. And, she did all this while having fun and while she was just a freshman.

INTERNSHIPS CAN HAVE
LONG LASTING BENEFITS

If the relationship grows, a summer intern will know the business from the ground up and will be a valuable applicant for a full-time job. In effect, the intern will have had ten weeks of basic training to sell back to the company which offered the program. The difference between a summer job in an organization and an internship is often just the name. Internships are sometimes summer jobs with low pay or no pay, but the key elements to look for are exposure to a particular field, company, and key persons. A formal internship usually allows for more exploration. Interns are there under the auspices of studenthood, rather than as part-time employees. This can make a big difference when it comes to overall exposure.

If you can pull off a summer job with some income attached and can accomplish the same objectives, so much the better. It's just that there are more low or nonpaying internships available, and by comparison, they naturally are easier to come by or create.

Internships are not designed to set you up for your life's work. They are best used as exploratory ventures to acquire background and insight otherwise unavailable to you. If the internship eliminates a job move or two in the first couple of years of your career, it will have contributed its worth in the saving of time and effort alone.

If the internship eliminates a job move or two in the first couple of years of your career, it will have contributed its worth in the saving of time and effort alone.

First job turnovers tend to be very high in the initial eighteen- to twenty-six-month period. The reason for the turnover most often is that the job isn't meeting the new employee's expectations. It is years later when many people realize that their expectations were not very sound to begin with. The low-risk internship will give you the necessary exposure to temper your expectations.

DO-IT-YOURSELF OR JOIN THE SUPERSTARS

Creating an internship from scratch is not as difficult as creating a job from scratch, although the procedure works along the same lines. The key ingredient is a contact person with the power to say yes. Ideally the contact person is also the person you will be working with, so select carefully. If you go too high in an organization or discipline, the experience will not translate back down to entry level. If you don't go high enough, you won't be dealing with enough authority to create a position. Also contact people can't be so busy

Don't apologize for contacts. Related ones are often the best kind.

that they don't have time to work with you, but they must be busy enough to have tasks that they can hand off to you. Be careful of research assignments in which you become a data processing clerk, although that might be a good price to pay in some cases. Ideally, you want interaction and maximum exposure.

Building your own internship usually requires several informational meetings, great chemistry, and a lot of luck to hit the right person. Don't cross off family contacts or the family contacts of friends. Doing it yourself is nice for the ego, but doing it is more important. Don't apologize for contacts. Related ones are often the best kind.

There are superstar programs which are sort of like miniature fast-track exposure trips, available from some larger companies. The objective in these programs is to give the participants a superficial looking over by a number of managers, as assignments are rotated every few days or weeks.

Superstar programs tend to be beauty contests and if you are beautiful they might be for you. Organizations often bring in large numbers of interns to screen for full-time employment a year hence; just by the nature of the process, they create more losers than winners. The benefit, of course, is that you have a name to trade on if you wash out. Make sure the name is a good one before you join a summer superstar ego trip.

Unlike the full-time job market which is slanted ninety/ten in the direction of unadvertised, unlisted opportunities, formal internship opportunities are almost always listed through someone in the college community.

If your college has a Director of Internship Programs, that's obviously the person to develop as a close personal friend. Contact, too, the National Society of Internships and Experiential Learning in Raleigh, North Carolina, which publishes a national directory of internships. The use of lead time is important because knowing a year in advance what's out there will allow you to do all kinds of things in preparation. You might want to make some informational fact-finding visits or better still meet with

> **Superstar programs tend to be beauty contests and if you are beautiful they might be for you.**

students who have participated in that internship before. Don't let these opportunities pass you by just because you didn't take the time to find out what's going on.

Some internships are offered only to specific schools or students with special backgrounds. These internships are often available to those who technically don't "qualify," so don't be afraid to prospect for internships through friends at other colleges. Ask them to see what has come into their coordinator. Once you know about an opportunity, there is nothing wrong with going after it

Putting your best foot forward doesn't work well if it's a paper foot that has kick me written on it.

directly. Many professors and instructors have contacts in the outside world, so it's not a bad idea to ask around to see if a source or name can be uncovered for follow-up.

Although some formalist advisor may tell you to send a resume as an opening move in going after an internship, it is just as poor a tactic in this effort as it is in a full-scale job search. Putting your best foot forward doesn't work well if it's a paper foot that has kick me written on it. (More about resumes later.)

Far better you send a note expressing interest, asking for a meeting, and giving minimal data. No one expects big backgrounds from students. Don't try to build a paper world for yourself. The odds are that you'll do more harm than good for your cause. Your objective is to get a meeting so you can find out what's involved, and so that you can be looked over. It's all subjective anyway, so why not just do it and go for it.

In an internship interview, you are just supposed to be wide-eyed, eager, and enthusiastic. You are playing a student. That's not a hard role. Cheat it a little on the side of being clean-cut and neat, but this is not a fashion show, so you can make a reasonable studentish appearance. Bring a list of questions concerning what other interns have done, and most important, ask all about the person who will be your supervisor. That's the person you should be interviewing with anyway, but if it isn't, you want to request a meeting. If it's a rotation program, this step will not apply; this is indicative of the reduced value of those kinds of set-ups. Take what they give you, but keep in mind what you would like.

Take what they give you, but keep in mind what you would like.

As a close to your meeting, ask what your chances are of getting the internship position. Then in a follow-up note be sure to say how good things looked. It's important to pin down a decision date because you need to finalize your summer plans as soon as possible.

Having sent an initial letter either as a meeting request or as a confirmation to an appointment is all that is necessary to establish a record of who you are, and to where and how you can be reached. A follow-up note after the interview will add to the impression you made and to your paper file. Just as in an actual job interview, the follow-up note must be personal, specific, and in the mail within 24 hours. Short and to the point with a reaction or some feedback is your objective.

By going after several internships, you will be building skills that will be very useful in your future full-scale job effort. These are your first opportunities for practice interviews in authentic situations so take advantage of them. Even the ones that don't materialize into internship offers will add to both your experience level and contact file.

Keep in mind that not much is expected, so it's difficult not to do well.

ONCE YOU'RE INSIDE

Once you are in your internship, it's open season to make as many contacts as possible. Start by keeping a daily journal. If you like to write prose, all the better, because your impressions and experiences will be a valuable framework for analyzing your evaluation of the workings of this kind of organization.

Write down the names and backgrounds of the people you meet. Not while they're standing there, but not too long afterward either. You don't want to lose anybody.

Asking questions is the primary skill you need to develop. If you have to write the questions down each day before you go in, that's OK, but don't waste a golden opportunity by letting the people and situations slip by in silence.

When you ask a question, listen, follow it up with another question, and listen some more. You will be perceived as a likeable, bright, and valuable student.

If you don't ask questions, you may be treated like a piece of furniture. Do what's asked of you, but ask, ask, ask, as much as you possibly can.

If you don't ask questions, you may be treated like a piece of furniture. Do what's asked of you, but ask, ask, ask, as much as you possibly can.

When you get answers, ask what they mean. When you come out of a meeting, ask what happened. When someone says something, ask them why they said it. This is the intern's prerogative. You're not supposed to know anything, so even if you do, just use it as a base for better questions.

Ask what you can read. Are there articles, books, manuals, reports, studies? Can you get a copy? What was the person's impression of the book? What should you look for? If someone is particularly helpful, don't be afraid to send a thank-you note.

Don't hesitate to continue to build your contact network, even while you are doing your internship. One student was going to study in England during the year following her internship. She questioned all of the international people she ran across for leads on a summer job with the company overseas. She received some good responses and a couple of letters of introduction for her trouble. Most importantly, people were pleased to try to help out.

Here, as in the work world in general, everything isn't necessarily a linear progression with one thing leading directly to another. The idea of exploring as many leads and avenues of opportunity as you can is what the internship challenge is all about. Wide eyes, questions, questions, questions, a big smile, writing down as much as you can interspersed with plenty of compliments to those around you . . . . that's the internship game.

After you have done an internship, you will begin to see the big difference between making a favorable impression with a high grade on a quiz or with a well-written essay, as opposed to making a favorable impression in the outside social world of people and organizations. The social world puts high priorities on a pleasant appearance, good conversational and listening skills, and a likeable personality.

Organizations require a person to wear well over an extended period of time. Learning to fit in is one of the new skills to develop.

> # Organizations require a person to wear well over an extended period of time.

CHAPTER 4

WHAT ARE YOU GOING TO BE WHEN YOU GROW UP ?

Narrow undergraduate specialization tends to produce narrow specialized people.

Early career choices are the "in" thing. Parents, professors, career officers, all like it when you make definitive statements on your career aspirations. There is only one problem. You have little or no data upon which to base your declaration. The question of what you are going to do is asked so often that it becomes almost a necessity to have an acceptable answer.

Saying that you are interested in nuclear marine bio-physics and that you intend to become a nuclear marine bio-physicist will usually allow the conversation to move onto another topic. Thus, specific career statements are often heard among college students.

In reality, most students have very little idea what they want to be in later life and considering their isolated academic environment, there is little reason to expect otherwise. The internship may help you focus on a possible career area, but just as likely, it will serve only to eliminate an area. Besides, it's that first-hand experience that makes internships invaluable.

THE MYTH OF THE
LINEAR CAREER PATH

It is common these days to have several careers. Preparing for all of them vocationally in college is unrealistic. Narrow undergraduate specialization tends to produce narrow specialized people. Being flexible and inquisitive for a few years can't do any real harm.

There is a belief that careers are highly linear and that at a certain age you must be at a certain stage. In some cases this reasoning can be justified, but there are many, many more careers that can be entered and left almost at will, at almost any time of life.

Informed career decisions are often made in the mid-thirties after a person has had a chance to look around for awhile, developing some likes and dislikes. From the mid-thirties on, career changes can be made at almost anytime. Your attitude should be flexible and open to ideas. Don't apologize for your spirit of exploration. At this stage, at any stage, it's healthy.

Don't apologize for your spirit of exploration. At this stage, at any stage, it's healthy.

Students are often influenced by the opinions and desires of others. One student was pre-med because, as he later reflected, his mother wanted a son to be in medicine. Eventually, he became a dentist and built a fine practice. It was hard work, but he did the best he could. He was in his late forties and rather committed to his life's work, when he understood why he had entered medicine and dentistry. It was easier to press on than it was to think in terms of a career change. He prospered until his retirement in his early sixties. When he finished his dental career, however, he became a new person. He learned to enjoy life, his family, and friends, and to relax, now that he no longer had to deal with the pain of others as a regular part of his everyday work.

Linear career paths are not all they sometimes appear to be. In the corporate world, everything seems to be a progressive pyramid. Did you ever stop to question the

> # The vast majority of pyramid climbers never get to the top.

shape and nature of a pyramid? The further you climb, the less space remains. The vast majority of pyramid climbers never get to the top. Many mid-life career crises are the result of coming to this realization in the mid-forties, after investing twenty years in what can be perceived as a losing linear progression career strategy. Again, the stereotype is often not as it seems. As a student, you usually have a few favorite courses, perhaps some academic aptitude in a specific area, an internship or two—if you were lucky—and informational interviews with some people in a career field. That's a little thin on facts for a lifelong career decision.

GET A JOB—NOT A CAREER

Gathering real career data actually begins after graduation when you begin to live in the work world and can make informed judgements based on your own experiences and the experiences of others. So your big jump into a first job isn't as big a jump as it may now appear. You are just looking for a place to begin looking. It's a paid education phase, if you like.

> **So your big jump into a first job isn't as big a jump as it may now appear. You are just looking for a place to begin looking.**

Seek the big opportunity if you want to, but it's not a life or death proposition. Contrary to popular belief, the big opportunity will come again and again for those who remain open to the possibility.

Your career treasure hunt will constantly supply all kinds of clues to what it is you want to "be." Some of them will be negative, pushing you out of areas unsuitable for you. Some will be highly positive in the form of friends and associates who will help you achieve things you probably never dreamed of doing yourself. It's all part of the hunt. Few decisions are forever. They can be, but even our dentist friend knew on some level that he had the option of doing things differently at any time. He kept his office in his house, limited the kinds of work he did, and treated himself to a compensating life-style that he felt was pretty reasonable.

> **Contrary to popular belief, the big opportunity will come again and again for those who remain open to the possibility.**

You can look at the logical progressions in careers from bottom to top when you are a student, but keep in mind things don't usually work out that way. You are better off basing your beginning decisions on the kinds of multiple career paths that are more common.

One student took a class in sales management that covered selling skills and included a day in the field with a sales representative. She didn't know whether this life would be for her, but it seemed to be worth a try. She was able to get a job in a small territory with an office services company that specialized in coffee and soft drink machines for businesses with under forty employees. Her sales manager was reasonable and it paid well enough for her to afford an independent life-style.

The work turned out to require twenty cold calls a day. Many of these came from telephone leads, but essentially they were cold calls. The product and service were good and she was able to meet her quota of four new accounts per week. That's four sales out of one hundred calls.

So what has this woman accomplished? She has decided that selling office services is not going to be her life's work. She has also discovered that doing this job every day has uncovered some strengths in persistence and discipline that she didn't know she had. Because she makes a good appearance and presents herself well, the principals in her accounts make her an average of two job offers a week. She is finding out that by being out on her own and getting a chance to see literally hundreds of businesses every month, she is beginning to get a sense of the opportunities available, something which no formal job search could uncover. (How could you visit one hundred prospects in a week?)

Where will this experience lead? She doesn't know. All she knows is that she is being paid, works on her own for a reputable company, for a reasonable boss, and is learning more each day. After six months in sales, she now handles herself with ten times the assurance of the student she was such a short time ago. Skills build rapidly when they are practiced and developed eight-plus hours a day.

Another student took a first job in the medical supply business. After earning his spurs in the field, he became assistant to a vice-president in the home office. He stayed in that assignment for five years. It proved to be a great learning experience. The V.P. shared his reasoning on every decision and the insights gained proved to be transferable to every company the junior executive worked with in the future. Sort of a five-year tutorial MBA with pay!

EVERY EXPERIENCE
A LEARNING EXPERIENCE

It is important in any developing career to find people who will teach and challenge you. They are often difficult to locate and sometimes you have to make do with a negative learning situation. When you get a marginal or poor manager to work for, you have to take it from another point of view. Assure yourself that when you get a chance to manage, you will not operate in the manner of your negative instructor and then observe what is done that is so destructive. Sometimes these negative exposures carry more impact from a learning standpoint than the steady, good example of a good manager, but they are wearing. If you are fortunate enough to find a dedicated and talented manager to work with, count your blessings and stay with that person as long as is practical and as long as it is a growth experience for you. If you are up against a less than talented boss, learn as much as you can, but get your moving plans in action as soon as possible. Waiting out situations usually takes far longer than anticipated. Moving on to a new challenge or a new organization can't be done quickly, so the sooner you begin the transition the better.

How will you know what career path to follow? Few people have the ability to design five-year plans and then make them happen. Reading biographies will give you a sense of the capriciousness of the process. Remember, though, biographies are only written about remarkable people. There are millions of people making their way through careers that will go unrecorded.

One biologist was hired as a lab technician to do simple infection testing on rabbits. It involved injecting the animals with a small amount of processed water and then monitoring for a temperature rise to indicate contamination. The company's owner had purchased an unused grain mill in a small country town, so our technician set up his lab and went to work. He had to sterilize his equipment and, therefore, had a small autoclave for that purpose. One of the firm's customers asked for some special packaged plastic sets. This assignment was sent up to the country lab, because that was where the autoclave was. The volume of special orders gradually grew and some assembly workers were hired to get the work out.

Several years later the biologist found himself running a production facility with over a hundred workers. A new building was required, so he purchased land and went into construction. The original company was sold, and our biologist quit. By this time he had acquired enough stock to afford a year off to travel across the country, while deciding what he wanted to do next.

When he returned from his travels, he was approached for help by one of the outside companies. He rented some old mill space and began again. This time,

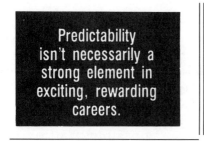

Predictability isn't necessarily a strong element in exciting, rewarding careers.

because he had been there before, the pattern for growth was laid out in advance, and it wasn't long before he was into construction of a modern facility. It included a first class testing laboratory, reflecting his technical beginnings. Several years later he was approached by an international concern wanting a U.S. subsidiary. This time he sold his company to them, staying on as the president for his distant owners.

Should you take a job as a lab technician testing rabbit temperatures in order to build your own multi-million dollar firm? Hardly, but this story serves as an example of the real unpredictable world, illustrating the great open-ended adventure we can all be involved in. Again the lessons in such an adventure are not easily distilled. Education, opportunity, the right boss at the right time, all play parts. Some elements can be managed and some can't. Predictability isn't necessarily a strong element in exciting, rewarding careers.

When someone asks you what you are going to be, don't throw up your arms in despair. Look at the positive side. It definitely is a great adventure. Mobility is much more a factor than many of us would like to acknowledge. Statistically we change jobs or assignments an average of every two-and-one-half years. That's a lot of flexibility.

By the way, the stability gained in a ten-year assignment is not as valuable as you might guess. From the inside of an organization, you may think that your longevity is appreciated, but often you are perceived several steps behind your current skill level because

Statistically we change jobs or assignments an average of every two-and-one-half years. That's a lot of flexibility.

people have kept past projects, impressions, and dealings in their minds. Those early first impressions remain firmly entrenched. It's easy to become pigeonholed in a long-term relationship. From the outside, a ten-year assignment or group of assignments with a single company may be evaluated, not on your sterling performance, but instead on the popular view of your corporation or industry. So if you made a major contribution in, let's say, the domestic steel industry, you would have the very difficult task of overcoming the declining image of steel, despite your personal achievements.

Exploration and flexibility are most important when beginning a career out of college. Long-term plans are unrealistic until you can see where the action is and who the players are.

> **Of even greater importance will be the mastery of organizational dynamics, often called office politics by those who do not accept the challenge.**

THE DYNAMICS WITHIN

You will pick up specialized skills in whatever field you enter because as mentioned, you will be working at them eight or ten hours a day. There is no need to worry about being able to contribute. Of even greater importance will be the mastery of organizational dynamics, often called office politics by those who do not accept the challenge. In reality, organizational dynamics are the ongoing development of social skills which everyone must master. These skills sometimes become the most important aspect of your career development.

An excellent primer in this area is Betty Lehan Harragan's book *Games Mother Never Taught You.* It has become a paperback classic in this often ignored phase of career development. When to move, when to stick it out, who to follow, who to get clear of, are the real questions of career dynamics. Once you understand that there are no sure formulas and that you will never have solid fail-safe answers, then the questions become a little easier to handle.

> **When to move, when to stick it out, who to follow, who to get clear of, are the real questions of career dynamics.**

Someone once said that you get paid for everything you do, you just don't know when. Don't be afraid to spend some time testing a number of different options. Don't be afraid to break the chains to follow a solid lead (or not so solid lead). There are economic and geographic constraints that come and go at various stages of every career. They just add to the challenge.

Moving early and often takes courage, but it has its rewards. Relocating across the country or around the world may or may not be your thing. Relocation is not necessary for either a challenging job or a long-term career.

If you want to find a company with some long-term prospects for you, all you have to do is select one whose home office is in the area you want to be in. That, of course, doesn't always work, but it's those kinds of informed choices that combine to make a workable mix for each step along the way.

Always think of yourself as self-employed. The responsibility for who you are and where you are going is ultimately yours. This gives you a healthier perspective on what sometimes appears to be the delegation of your fate and location to some organization. The philosophy that you must do as "they" ask if you are to progress is a self-serving message for management to impose upon employees.

> **Always think of yourself as self-employed. The responsibility for who you are and where you are going is ultimately yours.**

You, however, know better. You must always be developing Plan B—the outside option, the industry contacts, the ways of either staying put or going where you want to go. All the people you meet along the way— the intern acquaintances, the customers, those you met through informational interviews—should be maintained as active contacts. They may fit in your future in some strange ways, if you keep in touch with them. Being a little footloose at the beginning of a career is not all bad. Getting several years experience in several months time can be an exhilarating process. Being 100 percent committed to what you are doing allows for a steep learning curve.

One company had a unique approach to new employees. They gave each person a Mickey Mouse watch on the first day on the job. Employees were told that each time they looked at the watch, if they weren't having fun, they should consider giving it back and moving on. Working on the principle symbolized in the Mickey Mouse watch seems to be a much better philosophy than following the path symbolized by the gold watch.

It is a rare person who knows with real certitude what he wants to be and then follows that dream into the sunset for a lifetime.

It is a rare person who knows with real certitude what he wants to be and then follows that dream into the sunset for a lifetime. It is unrealistic to set that pattern as a standard.

Following the paths that you enjoy (once you discover them), working with the people who can help you or whom you can help, doing the things that you do best once you gain aptitude and skill are the fiber of most careers. These careers are far more dynamic than we are led to believe.

The famous career paths in the books are fun to read about. Creating your own as you go along is even more fun.

Every step is not critically important. Taking two steps forward and one back is more than acceptable.

> **Taking two steps forward and one back is more than acceptable. In fact, it's an indication that you are in control of the process.**

In fact, it's an indication that you are in control of the process.

When someone asks you what you are going to be, you can give them an honest and sincere answer along the lines of, "I will let you know as I begin to find out." Your first job is not only the starting point of your composite career mosaic, it is also the beginning of the process of learning more about yourself and how you will choose to fit in the world of work. It is definitely the beginning of an exploration and should be approached as such with an open mind, a willingness to look over many different trails, and a capacity to have fun while doing so.

CHAPTER 5

CONTACTS:
THEY ARE
EVERYWHERE

> *The antisocial indoctrination that has been beaten into you all these many years is the exact opposite of the social skills and gentle art of verbal communication you will need to survive and prosper in the outside world.*

Making, nurturing, and maintaining contacts is the central challenge of lifelong career development. You can't expect to be expert at the process on the first try, but skills in this area will begin to build with a little effort. Think about what you have been up against. As a student, you have been told not to talk to the person next to you. You have been encouraged to take notes, to go to some quiet place and study by yourself. In order to communicate, you have been asked to color in circles on multiple choice answer sheets. Now that technology has reared its ugly head, everyone is expected to be able to deal with a computer terminal in assorted languages. Trying to turn all this around in a few months time will not be easy. The antisocial indoctrination that has been beaten into you all these many years is the exact opposite of the social skills and gentle art of verbal communication you will need to survive and prosper in the outside world.

BUILD SOME SKILLS
BEFORE YOU NEED THEM

Begin by saying hello to those who sit on all sides of you in class. This will not be totally productive because they also have been programmed into silence, but they are safe to deal with in this kind of an experiment because you will not be called upon for any follow-up comments.

Next try for eye contact; a smile and hello to those you pass while walking on campus is excellent for practice. Again, don't worry about the responses because they will be few and far between. These are like stretching exercises. They don't add much to the skill base, but before you go out and try a heavy duty workout you would do well to loosen up a bit.

Make sure that you don't waste solid contacts because you lack the skills to take advantage of them once made. The sincere smile, the relaxed give-and-take, the dry-palmed handshake are impossible to fake. You must be doing all of these for as long as possible in order to be able to work well in the contact world. Someone in an active job search, trying to put all these fundamentals together for the first time, is a sad situation indeed. Begin your work on these elements at once. Remember, too, those subjective first impressions; you won't get to "show your stuff" if you never make it to round two.

One of the reasons that extracurricular activities are rated so highly by those who hire college graduates is that they are indicators of the ability to deal with multi-person social situations which focus on some kind of project completion. They duplicate to a lesser degree, the organizational environment you are entering. It matters very little what the extracurricular activity is, just so long as you are working with others to accomplish something.

WHERE DO CONTACTS COME FROM

The rule of 250 states that on average each person has about 250 friends or personal contacts within his or her family, social, or work circle. All of these are not viable business contacts, but with a certain amount of overlap each of your 250 persons has another circle of 250.

Your job in building contacts is to start looking for interesting leads around you. You can do this several ways and, in fact, should be working all methods at once.

Let's begin with your present circle of friends. More than one career has been launched by a roommate's parents. Just what do all these parents do? Do you know? It's not that you will be interviewed and hired by one of them, but they may be able to provide a name or lead in a direction worth looking into. This beats blind letters to Fortune 500 personnel departments (IBM gets 1500 unsolicited resumes a week). Your objective is to meet people with some life experience, and see if they will tap you into their contact network by giving you a referral or two. Your only obligation is a written thank-you note, and then a swift and professional follow through on the lead. It's usually a good idea to copy your source person on your follow-up notes to the leads they supply. Contacts of all kinds are part of the treasure hunt phase. You never know what will turn up, and you may not realize their value immediately.

THE UNIVERSITY CONNECTION

After you have worked over your own circle of college friends, you can take advantage of your university community connection in other ways. Even small colleges have alumni associations with the number of members running into the thousands. You have something in common with every one of them. Many alumni offices have print-outs by state that include job titles and work addresses. Printed alumni directories are published by many colleges.

Each year alumni return to campus for class reunions. Think of the opportunities available to you as an undergraduate, if you were to become involved as a student volunteer to help run some of these programs. Alumni love to be able to tell someone what it was like back then. In return for a listening ear, you can find out what they are doing now. It's then just a short step to ask how they arrived where they are, and you are off and running in an interesting life story, as well as an opportunity. Even if people worked in a particular field ten years ago, they often have contacts and friends who are still there.

A two-step approach could do the job for you. It's difficult to uncover a step-two person without taking step one.

This kind of give-and-take is best done at mealtimes or at social events, so plan on being on hand for these activities. Few students take advantage of this goldmine contact source. It's right there on campus for the taking, just by getting involved.

Many alumni have joined informational interview networks for current students as well as for fellow alumni. These network contacts can sometimes be found in special files set up for just this purpose. Again the fit may not be direct for what you think you might like to do, but the people that belong to the contact network could be just the kinds of people you need to give you that one good name from which to work. A two-step approach could do the job for you. It's difficult to uncover a step-two person without taking step one. Time after time undergraduates will hang their heads and say, "I just don't know what I want to do; I don't know where to begin." The answer is begin anywhere with contact names and find out what is going on. You won't believe how helpful they will be. You don't need a firm direction. All you need is the courage to begin. Your personal direction will evolve once you begin meeting with people and finding out what they do.

> *You don't need*
> *a firm direction.*
> *All you need is the*
> *courage to begin.*

TRADE AND PROFESSIONAL ASSOCIATIONS

Another source of contacts is trade and professional associations. Almost anyone who is anybody belongs to one or two professional associations. Sales and Marketing Executives International has chapters in most major cities. Students are always welcome to monthly programs at reduced rates. The programs are often developed around specific industries, but just as often they are cross-industry, focusing on specific disciplines. Meeting executives at a professional gathering, when they don't have all their screening devices in place, can be as easy as saying to someone before a luncheon break that you

> ## If you can name an industry or activity, it meets. And you can be there.

would like to meet "Mister Big." An introduction follows and, there you stand, face to face with someone who can do great things for you. You haven't had to write a letter, make a phone call, schedule an appointment, or do any of the things more formal contact methods require. The American Electronics Association will let you meet the Who's Who of High Tech. The National Society of Executives will provide a list of groups that is almost endless. If you can name an industry or activity, it meets. And you can be there.

Here is an example of a combination alumni-professional association approach that worked for one student. At a campus alumni meeting a student aide asked an alumnus who belonged to the National Society of Sales Training Executives for a contact in the consumer package goods field. A few days later, the student received a list of twenty consumer package goods sales training directors, all of whom the alumnus knew from his work in their professional association. The student went down the list, made a contact, and eventually landed a good entry-level job.

Two years later, now as a fellow, albeit junior, alumnus, our former student met his mentor at a university-sponsored luncheon. They discussed his career progress. He was doing very well and was being considered for a transfer and promotion to the home office. About a week later the senior man called and asked a favor. A client was going to be in town looking for some junior management talent, and would the young alumnus meet with him as a matter of courtesy just to fill out the visiting V.P.'s schedule? The favor resulted in an offer better than the home office promotion. You guessed it. The former student, junior alumni, junior manager took the offer; he is now three levels above that job and will have his own V.P. title shortly.

Back to professional associations and contacts. Many groups have local chapters and meet monthly. The business section of the Sunday paper usually has a schedule of these types of meetings. Most meetings will accept guests (even self-invited ones), so it's not as if you are crashing a party. That's how they attract potential new members, so everyone is welcome. Once you are there you can work the crowd for people you should meet. Arrive early and you can look over the badge table to see who is going to be there. Many times members of these groups will belong in order to do business with one another, so they are used to trading cards and making referrals. You may want to go to meetings repeatedly for a while, if you happen to strike a group that seems of value. Also don't forget the speaker. Presumably, he or she is smart enough to have something to offer the group, and it's amazing how approachable speakers are after making presentations. When the speaker completes his part of the program, several people usually want to talk with him, so all you have to do is wait your turn, and ask if you can meet at some future time with some specific questions about career opportunities.

When you call, say to the secretary or administrative assistant that you and your contact have talked briefly before and agreed to set up a meeting. You will be able to get more of these high-level contact meetings than you would imagine. It's just a question of going for it.

Trade meetings and conventions run year-round in every major city; again, a check of the business section will tell you who is in town. Registration fees sometimes run into the hundreds of dollars, so you will have to request a guest pass or student visitor tag. If you can't get into the main or breakout sessions without paying a big fee, then just go for a one-day pass into the exhibits. There will be a mix of industry suppliers and professional displays. Wandering around the booths provides an endless list of names, bags of literature, and a chance to meet face to face with industry practitioners. They even wear name tags with titles and locations, so you know who you are talking with. You can be as basic as asking just what they do in the industry. Ask, too, who the leaders, innovators, also-rans, big customers, important people, and sources of new talent are. Trade shows are great eye-openers, and the excitement can be contagious.

> *Don't feel as if you are out of place by being a student at a professional meeting. It is standard practice for students to visit many shows.*

Don't feel as if you are out of place by being a student at a professional meeting. It is standard practice for students to visit many shows. A three-day hospital industry show was attended by third day of exhibits every local student nurses on its year. The suppliers felt it was good future public relations to be helpful to the students. You needn't be a student nurse to make a visit to a medical show worthwhile, because every company in the medical field needs new talent in almost every discipline. This is true of almost all industry groupings—their needs are cross-discipline. Why not just go visit a random show or two regardless of the industry. They are great exploration grounds for new opportunities and for building probing skills.

Multi-day meetings often have evening social events, and if you can pick off an invitation or two to those kinds of gatherings, they are excellent opportunities for one-on-one informal meetings. Be careful of your social skills during these encounters because they sometimes involve open bars and lavish spreads of food. You should be polite and accept whatever refreshment is offered, but remember these social events must be handled well. Working a crowd at a hospitality suite is an art form in itself. They may look like parties, but they are in reality serious business and should be treated accordingly. Should you be asked, it's acceptable to say that you are attending the meeting doing industry research for yourself.

> *Working a crowd at a hospitality suite is an art form in itself. They may look like parties, but they are in reality serious business and should be treated accordingly.*

Equip yourself with business cards when you begin these informal face-to-face contacts, because it is the accepted method of exchanging names and follow-up data. Spend a little money on these cards because, as a student, a well-done card will single you out as an exceptional person. Nothing cute here, just straightforward and professional.

All of the rules of formal contacts apply at these gatherings. This means you should be very careful to answer questions with brief replies, and to ask as many questions as you can, keeping the conversational load heavily weighted on the other person's side.

Many times popular books have been written on an industry or a particular company. The titles may not be familiar to you, but if you ask an industry insider they may have two or three titles that will give you an in-depth view and a firm basis for questions. These are not all best- sellers, but for example: *Marriott, The J. Willard Marriott Story* by Robert O'Brien, (Deseret Books, 1981) will tell you something of the chain hotel industry. *I.B.M., Colossus in Transition* by Robert Sobel (Times Books, 1981) is a full history of computers in business. *The Wall Street Journal* by Lloyd Wendt (Rand McNally, 1982) is a 100-year history of Dow Jones, Inc.

The authors or the people mentioned in the books may be contacted for both direct information, possible face-to-face meetings, or for a referral to someone local of value to a student. Writing good request letters is a skill you must develop. Be very very brief. Ask for specific information. Identify yourself as succinctly as possible and follow-up all replies with both thank-you notes and prompt action on whatever is provided.

Contacts come from all sources. If someone is a guest lecturer or panelist at your college, that means the speaker has an interest in students, and is an accepted target of opportunity for your efforts.

Professors should not be ruled out, because they often have a wide circle of contacts and will give out a name or two if asked. Part-time university instructors, especially those teaching evening courses, are rich contact sources, because of their daytime practitioner status. It's not even necessary for you to take their courses. All you have to do is identify them and approach them for information and names.

All this means that you have to become a very forward person. There is no getting around the fact that careers require contacts from beginning to end. They just don't happen. They must be made to happen.

When someone gives you a referral, you are one step ahead, as there is no need to sell yourself to get your foot in the door. You are being seen in response to a peer professional's request. You must treat each referral with great respect and care, because invariably there will be some kind of feedback and you want it to be favorable.

> *Good things will happen in good time. There is no need to push a situation. Let it flow.*

> *Treat these networks with great respect, because you may want to go back to the well often.*

THE CIRCLE ALWAYS SEEMS TO COME BACK AROUND

Good things will happen in good time. There is no need to push a situation. Let it flow. If you think you have a hot lead or a live one you want to follow up aggressively, get back to your original contact who perhaps can make an inquiry as to how the situation stands. Treat these networks with great respect, because you may want to go back to the well often.

The major positive side to the contact network lies in your future value to a company. The person who referred you is credited for finding you, and thus the wheel of reciprocity and contacts continues turning. The essence of growth for all organizations is good people. Finding good people is a major task of managers, so you are a

> *Don't apologize for making an effort to meet people; it very well could be in everyone's best interests to sponsor you.*

> *Going for it on a one-on-one basis gives you a far better chance of doing yourself justice then trying to push yourself forward in the herd.*

potentially valuable asset even in the rawest form of raw material. Don't apologize for making an effort to meet people; it very well could be in everyone's best interests to sponsor you.

Going for it on a one-on-one basis gives you a far better chance of doing yourself justice than trying to push yourself forward in the herd, by taking conventional personnel interviews and recruiting routes.

There are thousands and thousands of contact opportunities open to just about everyone. The determining factor will always be a willingness to go after them. Skill in working over the field can be developed. The more you do it, the better your chances of making some hits. At certain levels and in certain fields, the contact network is the only option for growth. Keep in mind that this is a lifelong practice and the sooner you begin the better. Not having a contact network in good repair is like being on a ship without lifeboats. If the ship sinks, you're without options.

> *Not having a contact network in good repair is like being on a ship without lifeboats. If the ship sinks, you're without options.*

Pick out some of these sources and begin. Get a group of students together and work together for information and skills. Try a letter approach to an author who has written something of interest to you. Go visit a trade show. Find a professional meeting to attend. Any profession, any trade show, just do one. Being carefully focused at this point is not a necessity. Not doing something to begin to focus is a problem. Begin to see what is out there. You are going to be there very, very soon, so the quicker you get your contact act in operation the better. Do it for practice or for real, for fun or for profit, but do it.

> **Being carefully focused at this point is not a necessity.**

Start to build contacts through informational interviews, internships, and some of the many sources in this chapter. Most students don't have tightly focused career plans at this point. Don't worry about the specific goals; they will come sooner or later, as they do for almost everyone. If you accept the challenge of the business of getting jobs, the specific goals will come much, much sooner. Now, onto the process of selling yourself when you find something that looks like it's worth going after.

CHAPTER 6

SELF MARKETING: SELL THYSELF

> **You should always regard yourself as both self-employed and as a marketable service.**

Getting a job definitely is a business; think of yourself as self-employed with a deferred income. Self-marketing or selling yourself to the work world is a job in itself, the first job you undertake, and the most important job of all. In fact, it will be an ongoing job throughout your professional career. You should always regard yourself as both self-employed, and as a marketable service. You are selling yourself to an employer, and, if you make the sale, you have a new job.

All of the elements of the sales and marketing discipline go into the job-getting process, whether you recognize them or not. You will do market research in the form of informational interviews and internships. You may convert some of those same efforts into sales prospecting by following up on those leads or referrals which qualify as high, medium, or marginal potential employers. Each prospect, then, requires a specifically tailored selling strategy in accordance with the situation you discover and develop.

How can you say you are unemployed when you are doing all of this? It is hard work and the returns are definitely high stakes.

When you begin to generate offers, take a minute or two and project their cash value over a three- or five-year period. Add in a 40 percent fringe benefit factor and put in 10 percent increases for each year. The dollar value of the offer you are trying to close is substantial. You can't expect something of that magnitude to quickly fall into place just because you have arrived on the scene. It's not unusual for a professional capital equipment sales representative to spend six to nine months in pursuit of a sizeable piece of business. You can expect it to take almost as long for you to produce the same results.

> **The dollar value of the offer you are trying to close is substantial. You can't just expect something of that magnitude to quickly fall into place just because you have arrived on the scene.**

Your product is a good one. You are educated (soon to be made official by a degree), flexible, highly adaptable, energetic, eager, and ready to begin, and in demand because of the never-ending needs of the marketplace.

You are the marketing director and senior sales representative in your campaign to get a job and, therefore, you are very much employed. You will be paid substantially for your efforts; it's just that you won't start to get your money until you close your sale. Straight commission sales reps don't think of themselves as being employed only on the day they make a sale. They know that they must work every day in order to produce results down the road. You are in the same situation; the better job you do up front, the better the result you can expect.

Try to be as open as you can during the research and contact phase. You live inside the most adaptable organism on earth, and your directional limitations are relatively few. Not only can you do many things you have not thought of or trained for, but you may make future

> **You live inside the most adaptable organism on earth, and your directional limitations are relatively few.**

> **Finding the market area where you will have the greatest impact and produce the greatest return is a never-ending challenge.**

> **The more important the area of contribution, the more compensation you will be able to command.**

shifts as well. The product that we all market is very flexible and adaptable, if we choose to view it that way.

Finding the market area where you will have the greatest impact and produce the greatest return is a never-ending challenge.

Keeping an open mind is difficult when everyone is trying to fit you into tight profiles and career paths with specialized skills and backgrounds. Knowing that you can tailor yourself to do what you feel will bring the greatest return is a healthy personal view. The more important the area of contribution, the more compensation you will be able to command. Begin to focus not so much on industries and corporations, but what it is you do well, and enjoy doing. It's not the where (that will follow); it's the what.

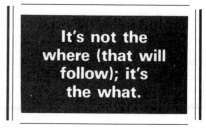

> **It's not the where (that will follow); it's the what.**

SELF-MARKETING SKILLS

Self-marketing requires packaging, display, and advertising. Positioning your product (you) is a major element, as is targeting your audience (employer).

Some divisions of organizations are, by their nature, more important, powerful, and visible than others. It is always a good idea to make an objective evaluation of the importance of a function to a company during the selection process. What is a key function in one company may be merely a support function in another, so where and how you market yourself may be critical to your future growth.

Being in support of a key function is not the same as performing the function. If you are going to be working hard anyway, it might as well be in the most important corporate area possible.

You don't have to become a hero or company savior, but by being selective in the area of your contribution, you can increase your visibility and return accordingly. Almost every discipline has pre-eminent value in some enterprise. Your job is to find the company where your contribution is of most value. This key consideration has long-term impact on your career growth, even given the exact same performance by you once on the job.

The purchasing function in the candy business, for example, is of major importance because of the wide price swings in chocolate. Profitability in that business is often a question of the skill of the buyers. In other high growth industries, purchasing, while important, is merely charged with being sure materials are available; they only achieve high visibility status when something goes wrong. In this case, if you think that you have an aptitude in purchasing, it is important to select a position in an industry which gives you a chance to show what you can do, and which appreciates what you can do. Market yourself to an industry where your skills are of primary importance.

Being in support of a key function is not the same as performing the function. If you are going to be working hard anyway, it might as well be in the most important corporate area possible.

Almost every discipline has pre-eminent value in some enterprise. Your job is to find the company where your contribution is of most value.

Another consideration must be the cyclical nature of all organizations to expand and eventually contract. The higher your value in the enterprise, the greater your reward, and the more critical your talent in a cutback. It is also more likely, if you are in a central rather than support position, that you will have the time and information to read a declining situation, deciding whether to wait it out on that particular ship or move on while still in a position of power.

You can often gain visibility by either joining or being attached to new ventures. This involves some career risks, but risks are everywhere and not seeking risks can be hazardous in itself. There is a fine line in visibility and self-promotion. Push it too far and you're viewed negatively. Don't push it far enough and you are invisible.

The higher your value in the enterprise, the greater your reward, and the more critical your talent in a cutback.

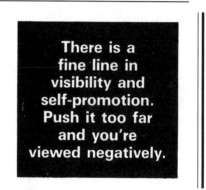
There is a fine line in visibility and self-promotion. Push it too far and you're viewed negatively.

There are some rewards in being a secret agent, but be sure that is what you have decided to be, and not just the consequence of working in a backwater area. On occasion, during reorganization and power shifts, anonymity can be of value, but being where the action is generally carries appropriate rewards.

In some situations, the understated team player is valued. That is a very difficult game to play, because it is hard to demonstrate value if you are hidden somewhere in a pack, dependent upon the good will and fair judgement of some superior for your market value points. The earlier you can gain individual visibility, the better. Market yourself where there is room to extend your reach, and where you can keep yourself fluid and flexible. Now is the time for these considerations, before you've landed your job.

> **Those who discount appearance, take refuge in performance which they hope will be recognized. It's not an either-or situation. It's a question of covering all bases.**

> **When you are face to face with anyone in the hiring cycle, you are in a selling situation. For the most part, you are selling a service product and a relationship rather than hard qualifications.**

LOOKING THE PART

You can improve your packaging with careful dress and grooming. Having a sincere suit for an interview is just the beginning. The packaging challenge gets more important as you go along. Appearances count heavily and investments in appearances are not frivolous. Those who discount appearance, take refuge in performance which they hope will be recognized. It's not an either-or situation. It's a question of covering all bases. Visuals are important. Setting high quality standards for your personal performance and appearance is a marketing element that will pay off sooner than you might think.

Looking the part has two positive returns. First, it builds your own confidence and actually tends to increase performance quality. Second, you are perceived by others as either having ability or potential ability by how you look. Many people perform well in the midst of a mess, yet it is almost certain that they are perceived by others as being more capable when they pay attention to the externals of packaging and overall appearances. The carefully indexed report with tabs and cover sheets is perceived to be of more value than the same data sent along in worksheet form. The performance may be the same, but it's the little extra marketing step that counts.

> **Be careful not to get into a presentation mode. It is the least productive posture.**

EACH MEETING IS A SALES CALL

When you are face to face with anyone in the hiring cycle, you are in a selling situation. For the most part, you are selling a service product and a relationship rather than hard qualifications. Professional sales people ask many, many questions and pride themselves on being able to adjust and adapt to situations. This is the task you face. It's just an extension of the informational interview process already discussed. The stakes are a little higher, and you no longer have the cover of being a student doing career research.

As a self-marketer (applicant), you still want to draw out maximum information, rather than revealing too much. When sales professionals let the customer do all the talking, they find their jobs easier and positive results more likely. Be careful not to get into a presentation mode. It is the least productive posture. Saying that you are interested is a weak statement. Being excited, anxious to get going, enthusiastic, wanting to make a contribution, are the selling signals that contribute to positive responses.

Your overall self-marketing program must be people-focused. The human elements are the ones that decide your fate, and they are also the most important factors in narrowing your prospect list.

A flow chart of your self-marketing activities will begin with market research leading to market identification, next to segmentation, and then to prospecting, and finally to sales. Some of these activities will overlap but the structure can be seen without difficulty.

The one element not covered in your self-marketing program is your sales literature and materials (resumes). This is so important and so misused that it deserves a separate chapter. Resumes have a place, but it's not the one everyone assigns to them. Let's take a closer look at just what resumes can, can't, should, and shouldn't do.

CHAPTER 7

DANGER! RESUMES CAUSE CAREER DAMAGE

> **From first job right on through to the president's chair, the resume is the document that does the most damage and the least good.**

> **The resume is nothing more than a big sign that says kick me. It then goes on to provide the size 12 boot with which to do it.**

> **Resumes are a double-edged negative sword. Not ony do they separate good people from the opportunity to present themselves for possible positions, but they give power to credentials and past experiences which have little or nothing to do with the challenges of actual future tasks.**

Getting caught in the resume trap is one of the most common errors in career management. From first job right on through to the president's chair, the resume is the document that does the most damage and the least good.

The resume is nothing more than a big sign that says kick me. It then goes on to provide the size 12 boot with which to do it. Resumes have only one practical use for a potential employer. They are a means to screen out, eliminate, reject, separate, and reduce the number of candidates for jobs.

"One does not willingly fashion a club with which to be beaten." One would think so. Millions of people not only do that, but a whole cottage industry has sprung up to help them do it. Typists, quick copy shops, consultants, and a library of specialized literature are all dedicated to the construction of resumes. Unfortunately, they will accomplish the exact opposite of their intent; they screen people out of opportunities.

Resumes are a double-edge negative sword. Not only do they separate good people from the opportunity to present themselves for possible positions, but they give power to credentials and past experiences which have little or nothing to do with the challenges of actual future tasks.

Even worse, people make career decisions based on how something will look on a resume.

Think of it this way. Let's say you are a bridge builder and you have heard that a city or town is going to contract for a new bridge. Would you send in a bid before you were able to get the specifications? When you received the specs, would you send in a general bid that you use for all bridges? Crazy! Without detailed information, it would be impossible to prepare an intelligent bid. The fact that everyone else is sending in general bids just increases the lunacy.

On the other side of the desk, you hear constant moans about the difficulty of going through all these meaningless bids (resumes). The whole resume sham is totally out of control. Do everything possible to stay out of the resume pile.

Start by not having a prepared resume. If you don't have one, you can't give it to anyone. If you don't have one, you can't send it in to anyone. If you don't have one, you must do something else when asked for a resume.

When presented with this approach, almost everyone agrees with its logic, but few are prepared to be strong enough to come up with good answers and workable alternatives to the inevitable resume request. Most just shrug their shoulders and give in with their little personalized kick me signs.

If some interviewer said to you, "Well, you seem to fit pretty well; now, please take off all of your clothes," you would have a couple of polite answers along the lines of that not being appropriate.

Every time we casually comply with a resume request, what we are doing is supplying all kinds of subjective irrelevant data.

The hiring process is subjective enough without submitting to the indignity of a nude inspection. And yet, every time we casually comply with a resume request, what we are doing is supplying all kinds of subjective, irrelevant data upon which some kind of judgement will be pronounced. Hobbies: Bowling—"must be a late-hours beer drinker." Extra curricular activities: Chess Club— "never did understand that game." Born: Los Angeles— "We haven't had much luck with southern California people." And on, and on, with at least one subjective negative for almost every fact you can list.

Whenever you are asked for a resume, just remember that you are being asked to take off your clothes. You may have nothing to hide; it's just that it's not a useful request and can only be used against you.

Whenever you are asked for a resume, just remember that you are being asked to take off your clothes. You may have nothing to hide; it's just that it's not a useful request and can only be used against you.

DEFLECTING RESUME REQUESTS

It's not practical to indignantly leave the room whenever you are asked for a resume, so you must learn to deflect those requests. Substitute an after-the-fact letter of interest and qualifications which provides a document of relevant data with which to open your file.

When deflecting a request this way, ask who the manager is for this particular job, or who will be making the hiring decisions. You may be given a general response, but your request might lead you to the key person. Then your carefully targeted response takes on new meaning. It never hurts to ask. You are allowed to ask questions at all times. (Students are allowed almost an infinite number, so take advantage of your privileged position.)

In preparing an alternative response to a resume, ask for the job title and a formal position description. Ask what the job requires, so that you can match your background against it. Ask for a profile of the ideal candidate. Although you may not have all the job qualifications, you may have some that are considered very important. And, too, you can begin to see how to sell yourself and whether this job makes best use of your strong points. All of this data is best gathered in person, so an informational meeting is obviously required before you can prepare any kind of reasonable alternative response.

Now you can begin to see how this all fits together. Contacts and informational interviews keep you informed so you can determine where and if you want to fit, all the while giving you exposure for a one-on-one decision if things look positive.

Deflecting resume requests and turning them into informational meetings is not easy. Many top professionals don't have the courage or skill to do it. The reason it is mentioned here is not to make you an outlaw before you begin, but to sensitize you to this concept of not eliminating yourself from jobs before you even find out what is going on. Many people who work at the business of getting jobs without a resume find that it is no big deal when they are face to face with someone. The no-resume problem comes with advance requests over the phone or when someone says send me two or three copies so I can distribute them. At this point, say that you are not that far along yet, and you would just like an informal meeting to ask some questions rather than a formal interview. Of course, you really want the names of key people for face-to-face contacts; you don't want resumes flying around, getting in your way by preventing you from making an in-person first impression.

A CAREER SCAPBOOK

While you want to avoid a resume and shouldn't even have one, you do need a sound data file of all the meaningful things you have done in your life, along with the key dates, and if possible, documentation and photos. You can even do a miniautobiography. It will help you get to know yourself better. You'll begin to see recurring areas of interest. (Perhaps you thought you were interested in theatre, when actually it is construction (of sets) that fascinates you.) In any case, this file is your personal, unbiased resource, not to be disseminated indiscriminately to every personnel office on the coast!

> A scrapbook-file is your personal, unbiased resource, not to be disseminated indiscriminately to every personnel office on the coast!

> **The trick to an alternate response is to make it lean and specific. Go with whatever strength best applies and leave out all the detail that is peripheral.**

> **Remember that key factors in every job match are a person's desire to do the job and the enthusiasm in selling that desire.**

Start a career scrapbook in the beginning, because it will be invaluable as you go along. This idea comes out of the advertising industry where creative people keep a portfolio of their work, which they can then show to prospective employers. These visuals are great selling tools, and it's not hard to pick up visual samples of many of the things you do, if you are smart enough to look for them and save them. A newspaper clipping when cut out, mounted, and copied is a great selling piece. If a photo goes with it, even better. It needn't be out of the *New York Times.* Just the fact that it's typeset and printed adds impact and authority. Clippings from school papers or from event programs will start your collection off. A big old scrapbook is a great resource, but you have to be on the look-out for things to put in it.

With all of these dates, places, events, and support materials, you now have the data base to make specific responses to individual requests. No blanket resumes for you!

The trick to the response is to make it lean and specific. Go with whatever strength best applies and leave out all the detail that is peripheral. If, for example, the potential job requires a relocation commitment you can include in a follow-up letter a list of all of the places you have lived or traveled to. Why should someone have to try and dig all of that out of a resume that most likely wouldn't have it listed anyway. You do the screening and send only what fits.

Remember that key factors in every job match are a person's desire to do the job and the enthusiasm in selling that desire. Enthusiasm is almost impossible to get on paper. Desire is difficult to sell over the phone. Therefore, you must make a great effort to deflect requests for resumes, and instead turn them into actual meetings.

It obviously can't be done every time and if after all else fails, you decide to send something in print, go to your data file, scrapbook, folder, or whatever, and select your one or two key qualifications for this particular contact. Take the top one and lead with that in your response letter, back it up with your other, then push as best you can for a follow-up meeting.

Work hard to be concise. A one-page letter should suffice. If not, go back and trim some more. Again, as in marketing, you have but a moment to grab someone's attention.

If you are sending support material use a large envelope and send everything flat. Make it look good. Try not to send originals of anything. But, if you choose to use originals to backup your ideas, that's just one more reason to meet in person (so you can pick them up).

All this may seem like an incredible amount of effort to go through just to get around a simple request for a resume, but if you stop and think what happens to resumes (and you as a result), it makes perfect sense to stay out of that self-destructive game.

HOW RESUMES DON'T WORK

Most people, most of us, can do almost anything if we have to. If we are motivated and are given a little help and support, there are, in fact, few things that we cannot do. Adaptability is the salient human trait.

Let's take a look at what the hiring process really is. A business is either buying your experience or buying your potential. Buying experience is a valid strategy for business, but it is, after all, only experience, and it's not always what it seems to be. Buying potential can be just as risky, but it usually is less costly, at least up front.

The problem is that almost every set of experiences must be modified or tailored in some way to fit a new environment. The people-chemistry equation is an unknown factor in every new relationship, so all of this background-matching, especially on paper, has limited

> # The resume is, at best, only useful for background-matching or, in actual fact, to indicate the lack of same.

value anyway. The resume is, at best, only useful for background-matching or, in actual fact, to indicate the lack of same.

What you want to provide are one or two strong reasons why you and an employer should get together—not the reason why you shouldn't meet. Let's look at what happens to resumes.

Typically resumes are screened for red flags or knockout factors. If a manager gets in a hundred resumes, he or she can't study them, so they are sorted.

They begin with A, B, and C piles. It's a subjective scan, not a careful reading. (All colored paper goes into the C pile for some managers.) After they have three piles, a quick run through the Bs, gets one or two into the As, and then a rank order of the As gives them the people they want to talk with. Some managers then do telephone screening to eliminate those who don't sound very strong in responding to set questions. Can you imagine your twenty-year career with X. Y. Z. Co. getting short-circuited over the phone due to a bad connection where they hear you just fine, but you can't hear them?

Finally they decide to meet face to face with those in the top of the A pile. Is it any wonder that this process more often than not turns up marginal candidates for jobs? (Or at the very least eliminates some very able people for no good reason.)

Nowhere in this paper and telephone exercise can a realistic evaluation of a human being be made. As the saying goes, "it isn't fair." True. So what can be done about it? You are not in a position to make the system fair, but you are in a position to resist getting caught up in it.

Many people agree with most of this, but then they come up with a two-part, self-defeating strategy. They say, "Well, I don't believe I can win with a resume, but if that's what they want I have just as good a chance as anyone else, and rather than make waves, I will send one along. At the same time, I'll make every effort to do the right thing and go after the information contacts and try for the face-to-face meetings that I know are harder to get, but are much more productive."

The fact is this two-part strategy just eliminates a large number of potential jobs and increases the rejection rate, taking up your valuable time, with only an outside chance of anything reasonable resulting.

In fairness to the system "that isn't fair," it must be admitted that some jobs do result from this approach. It's just that it's so arbitrary. If you have what it takes to penetrate this kind of screen, you could do at least as well, or more likely much, much better by going at it from the contact approach, and thus completely avoiding the resume maze. What's more, you are apt to end up with a job which is a much better match all around when a resume hasn't been part of the process.

Resumes keep you from any kind of innovative job search. With a resume, you can never get ahead of the game, by going after positions which don't yet exist, because so much personal selling is required in landing these positions. They never materialize without the up-front information-gathering, relationship-building, and positive energy needed to move a good idea to a concrete offer.

At any stage of your career, resumes destroy individuality. Even if you are approached for a position because of your unique qualifications, a resume can spell disaster. As soon as you produce a resume, you become yet another applicant. Once you are an applicant, you are worth 20 to 30 percent less in cash than someone not officially in the applicant pool. In other words, when they come after you, they must give you all kinds of incentives

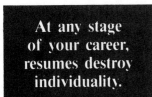

At any stage
of your career,
resumes destroy
individuality.

and cash to get your attention. When you flash a resume, you decrease your value by saying, "It's not going to take much to get me; I am all ready to go." The damage is incredible, yet people insist upon shooting themselves in the foot on a regular basis.

Not only do they do it, but they use hollow tipped bullets as well.

Resume terminology is so convoluted,it is meaningless. People go to great lengths to encode their lives into unbreakable resume language. The amount of effort and expense that goes into creating these tools of self-destruction is beyond all logic and reason. You only have to read through a pile of fifty or sixty of them at one sitting to get the feeling of futility and non-communication they produce. It's almost impossible to remember that these destructive pieces of paper represent real, live human beings.

Trying to take your past and describe it in such a way that it will somehow fit both an unknown future and the subjective screening process of some unknown person is surely one of the great long shots of all time.

What is of importance is not your past, but your future.

Did you ever watch the television weather with rising impatience waiting for the forecast, while millions of dollars of computer graphics and toothy grins explained

When you flash a resume, you decrease your value by saying, "It's not going to take much to get me; I am all ready to go." The damage is incredible, yet people insist upon shooting themselves in the foot on a regular basis.

> **Trying to take your past and describe it in such a way that it will somehow fit both an unknown future and the subjective screening process of some unknown person is surely one of the great long shots of all time.**

what went on that day. You lived through today's weather and you could care less about it with only minor exception. What you want and need to know is what the prediction is for tomorrow. All you need is one little slide. Is it going to be good or bad? Rain or shine? How good or how bad? You will then take a chance. Things change, but you accept that.

How many times have you sat through "the weather" and because of all the irrelevant production actually missed the forecast?

The minute details of your background and experience are of little interest to anyone except you. What counts is your future, and you want control over that. What are your plans? How will you fit? Where will you fit? Are you worth taking a chance on? Fight the resume battle as hard as you can.

Send out only dated and personally addressed written material. Provide only tailored and detailed data in response to qualified requests. By volunteering little, all you can do is raise interest. Every piece of material you send out should be a typed original. Your letterhead should be the only professionally printed element.

If you want to send support material from your scrapbook, be sure it fits closely, shows you in the best possible light, is clean and professionally reproduced, and is not overkill.

When someone says to you send us a bid on any old bridge, take off all of your clothes, or send me a resume, you should have a good, prepared answer and strategy in readiness, and you should practice a smooth delivery and polite comeback. "I'll send a letter of interest this afternoon. Is there a specific position I should tailor it for, or qualifications I should highlight? I'm still in the information gathering stages right now, so I don't have a prepared resume, but I'll send a little background letter." (With as little information that can be used against me as possible.) You can't change the system, but there is no need to play the game by someone else's rules.

CHAPTER 8

WHAT INTERVIEWS ARE ALL ABOUT

> *Simply stated,
> the more they talk,
> the better you are
> doing. The more
> you talk, the less
> your chances of
> being successful.*

During a home office round-robin interview, an applicant was guided from one executive to another by a personnel manager.

Early in the afternoon of this one-day extravaganza, the applicant was ushered into a senior vice-president's office. After brief introductions, the guide left, and our applicant did his best to respond to questions, tell his story, and survive the encounter. The job in question was entry level, requiring twelve weeks of indoctrination in Chicago, and then relocation to some other part of the country (unnamed until after the first twelve weeks). Not the best possible deal, but for this time in our applicant's life, he felt it to be a reasonable opportunity.

As a conversational qualifier, the V.P. asked if there were any parts of the country the applicant would prefer. Naturally enough, being from the Northeast, the applicant said he would be most comfortable in a northeastern location.

The follow-up question was logical enough; the V.P. wanted to know if there were any areas of the country that would be on the bottom of the list, just to be sure that the best possible match would result. The applicant said that having spent several months in Texas at one time, he felt it would be the one place he would not like to return to.

Fair enough. Still in a friendly manner the V.P. asked about the Texas experience. The next fifteen minutes revolved around hot, dry weather, endless stretches of highways, oil refineries, Mexican border towns, and the "hurry on back now" goodbyes heard at every stop.

Finally the conversation shifted back to job qualifications, and then time was up. The personnel manager reappeared, and they were off down the corridor for the next interview.

The first question asked as they rounded the corner was, "Well, how did you make out with Tex?" And so, that company lost a good potential employee on the basis of the hometown bias of a dyed-in-the-wool Texan, who for some strange reason didn't sound like one.

What could our applicant have done? There's lots he could have done to tip the scales in his favor. Even so the whole interview process is so abitrary that in spite of all kinds of skills and preparation, funny little things often pop up and destroy the best of plans and strategies.

There is, however, an approach to interviews which takes advantage of the natural flow of the encounter. If you understand how that works and can practice some basic skills, it will increase your chances of getting more positive results from interviews. By shifting an evaluation or job interview into an informational interview, you gain all kinds of points in two areas. First, you develop data that will help you respond to future questions more specifically and, second, and most important of all, you build a more positive personal relationship with the interviewer.

Simply stated, the more they talk, the better you are doing. The more you talk, the less your chances of being successful.

WORKING THE INTERVIEW TO YOUR ADVANTAGE

Evaluation or first interviews are not the best ways to pick employees nor are they the preferred way for you to pick a potential organization or boss. They are strained encounters which many managers don't handle well. They use patterned questions, stress, personal probes, and all kinds of counterproductive and often unprofessional methods. You will find after a few interviews that there aren't many good interviewers. That's unfortunate, but it's not your problem.

> **The interview may lead to a job, but there are many intermediate steps along the way; by working on each step, you increase your chances of reaching your ultimate goal. Don't get ahead of yourself.**

If you take a little different look at that sorry situation, you can see an opportunity to turn it around to your advantage. You will have a chance to take many interviews, and just the repetitive nature of the process gives you a chance to build some impressive skills, if you know what your objectives are. So, even the greenest student can increase his of her interview ratings by understanding the dynamics and the specific objectives.

Easy you say, but what you want is a job. Yes, but that is not the purpose of an interview. The interview may lead to a job, but there are many intermediate steps along the way, and by working on each step, you increase your chances of reaching your ultimate goal. Don't get ahead of yourself. Stop and ask the question one more time. What are you trying to accomplish with this one evaluation interview? Now you begin to look at short-term results. What will happen if this interview is successful? Most of the time, it will result in another interview. Now the objective becomes clearer—to meet again. That's totally different from trying to get a job, and, therefore, your approach and strategy change. Preparation for an interview isn't a library research project. It's a focused effort to work towards a single predictable result. Meeting again is the primary objective of evaluation interviews from your perspective.

What are some of the reasons an interviewer might want to meet someone a second time? He likes you. He wants to learn more about you. He wants someone else to meet you. He wants to show you something that wasn't available at a first meeting. He wants to help you. He wants to give you more information. He wants to explain more fully what's involved. All of these reasons are good ones for getting together again. See how it works, or rather how you can make it work for you. Keep your foot in the door, learn more about the opportunities, and reveal as little about yourself as possible. No resume. Face-to-face meetings. A chance to sell yourself.

If you focus your interview efforts on achieving your objective (meeting again), your chance of accomplishing what you set out to do is greatly increased.

> **You can almost be certain that your first meeting is what is called a "white socks" interview. At these meetings you simply have to avoid shooting yourself in the foot (through your white socks).**

THE "WHITE SOCKS" INTERVIEW

Setting a realistic objective in advance gets you moving towards that objective. You can almost be certain that your first meeting is what is called a "white socks" interview. At these meetings you simply have to avoid shooting yourself in the foot (through your white socks). It is an inspection-type, get-acquainted visit to see if the applicant has two heads, wears white socks, or displays idiosyncrasies that will identify him or her as a little too different to bother with.

One of your first meeting objectives is to find out about the normal interview cycle in this organization in order to set a workable objective and strategy for the next meeting. This is not secret information; in fact, some interviewers volunteer it, but others don't think it important and, therefore, you must ask for it. If it is volunteered, you can ask follow-up questions to gain more data with which to work on your next move. Intelligent questions along these lines will give the impression you know what you are about. What more could you ask en route to your next or second meeting?

> **Contrary to popular belief selling is not telling.**

> ## The art of interviewing for a job is exactly the opposite of what is normally perceived. You interview them —not the other way around.

Contrary to popular belief, selling is not telling. Presentation skills are not interview skills. You are always selling when you are meeting with people who can do things for you. The most valuable skill in selling yourself is the ability to build a one-sided dialogue. Your role is to keep the ball in the other person's court. If you can get a 90/10 ratio (they are speaking 90 percent of the time) of communication, you can't lose.

The art of interviewing for a job is exactly the opposite of what is normally perceived. You interview them—not the other way around.

The techniques are very similar to the informational interview. It's open book, it's go through your list of questions, it's take notes, it's make your own answers brief.

If you want to show someone how smart you are, you must ask a smart question to which they can give you a smart answer. Telling someone how bright you are is self-defeating. Making the interviewer feel good about himself—and therefore you—is the name of the game.

There is a power relationship in all interviews, so you must learn to go with the flow. This is more difficult to do if the interviewer is someone with minimal skills and talent, but if he has the power to say no, or not to pass you on, you must be realistic enough to recognize this fact and adjust accordingly. Just because an organization has an inept first interviewer is no reason to strike the company off your list. You may want to fix that problem when you get to be a vice-president, but the task at hand is to accomplish your preplanned objective, that next meeting.

People don't like to be blown away, so if you have the guns to do it, you had best keep them out of sight. You may be sitting there with your 3.7 average, all kinds of letters of recommendation, in your sincere suit, facing someone who doesn't appear to be very well organized. Back-off. Read the situation. Begin your questions. Take your time to find out what's going on.

Think about Tex. What a simple matter it would have been to get Tex talking about Texas instead of the way it turned out.

> ## *People don't like to be blown away, so if you have the guns to do it, you had best keep them out of sight.*

> ## *The whole trick to interviews, to selling yourself, is not to sell, not to interview, but to let the other person buy, to let the other person answer your questions.*

THE QUESTION OF QUESTIONS

The whole trick to interviews, to selling yourself, is not to sell, not to interview, but to let the other person buy, to let the other person answer your questions.

Many times an interviewer will make some kind of an opening statement. No matter how clear or straightforward it may be, you should come up with several follow-up questions as a result. If they say something as innocuous as "it's a nice day today," your comeback could be, "Do you come from this part of the country (Texas, maybe)?" or, "Do you like this kind of weather?" If you can come up with ten questions from a "nice day" lead, think of what you should be able to do with something more substantive.

If you are fast on your feet, wonderful, but it's not necessary. You can list pages of questions, and keep them right in front of you. If, after a few interviews, you find some questions and comments work better than others, begin to go to your strong suit as soon as you think it appropriate. The principle you are working on is show, not tell. Good questions show you at your best; telling about your achievements appears self-congratulatory and empty.

If you ask an obvious question or two, it's not that important because in some ways it's expected. It might even loosen up the interview a bit, and further support the interviewer's power position as being extra smart and in control.

There are three basic types of questions you want to develop. The first is a set of informational questions; this will be your longest list. The second is a set of directional questions; these will be designed to lead into some of your areas of strength.

"Is IBM/360 technology still in use in your organization?" This directs the discussion to further follow-up directional questions in your area of hoped-for strength. If the answer is no, then the come-back question is along the lines of, "What are you doing in that area?" If the answer is yes, the follow-up question will be "What are some of the applications you are involved with?"

Those are good directional questions, keeping the ball in the other court. However, avoid the blunders of the inexperienced candidate making statements about having used an IBM/360 in some project or other. The interviewer might then ask follow-up questions to probe the depth of the experience. Invariably the bullets begin bouncing off the floor as you try several shots at your foot.

Don't make statements. Ask questions. When you ask a good question and hit a live vein of information, be careful that the subject isn't turned back to you for a foot shot.

**Don't make statements.
Ask questions.**

Don't give back a sale. When you achieve your objective, take it and run.

"You seem to know something about data processing. Tell me about your project."

Don't. Just deflect it a little, and get back to what's important, which is what is going on with the company you are interested in.

"It was a market research case study. Do you use computer simulations in your market research group?" (Nice deflection.)

The third and final type of question is called a closing question and can be asked almost anytime during an interview, if the vibrations are positive. "How am I doing?" is a great closing question. It's sometimes called a trial close because you seek positive feedback on how to adjust the situation. A more formal closing question would be along the lines of, "What do you think? Am I worth a second interview?"

They might just say yes. At that point make an appointment, set a date, get whatever detailed information on the meeting you will need, and move out. Don't give back a sale. When you achieve your objective, take it and run. The world is full of people with stories to tell of how they had something all locked up, stayed around for a few more exchanges, and lost everything they had gained.

Closing questions are sometimes difficult to ask because they may result in some negative feedback. Regard them as opportunities to repair any negative vibrations you have. It's best to have closing questions written down in advance, so you will have the courage to actually ask them.

As you get further along in the interview process, closing questions gain in importance. Getting an offer, which is usually the objective of the final interview, requires strong closing techniques. When you learn to close, you send a message of being in control of yourself and your environment. It's a good impression to make.

> **You are looking for another meeting, not a job—at least not at first.**

> **You are trying to make friends with someone, whether you like him or not.**

> **You never want to just present yourself to be looked over. That leads to being worked over.**

A strong close which hasn't been preceded by good informational and directional dialogue won't do much good, but not to close after solid exchanges leaves things hanging in the air, causing feelings of uncertainty on both sides.

So, the interview process is one of dialogue, not presentation. You are looking for another meeting, not a job—at least at first. You are trying to make friends with someone, whether you like him or not. Your objective is for them to like you personally, and then professionally. You will, of course, always be evaluated as a person first, because few people will want you around on a permanent basis or will bring you in to meet their boss unless you are personally acceptable in their judgement. (Whatever that may be!) The second factor will be your technical qualifications, or in the case of entry-level positions, your perceived potential to do the job.

Get interviewers to respond to your preplanned questions which in turn lead them toward these preplanned objectives. The "How did you get here?" informational questions, which are easily answered, tend to establish your likeability if done well. Technical (directional) questions, which are about the opportunity or industry, will begin to show your potential. The more contacts and interviews, the better your questions will become.

It is not a bad idea to write your objective at the top of your question list, so that you don't lose sight of it in the heat of the exchange. You are always trying to accomplish an objective. You never want to just present yourself to be looked over. That leads to being worked over.

SHARPENING YOUR SKILLS

Go to a little trouble to have your tools look professional. Get a writing folder to carry with you. Make it leather, if possible, instead of vinyl. Carry it around to class and out in the rain for a few weeks to season it a little. Get a pen that isn't disposable. Use it for awhile. One candidate took out a new Cross pen and couldn't get it to write, because he didn't know you had to twist it to get the ballpoint out of the holder. Funny in print, but not so funny when it happened.

Much of this is easy to understand and describe; the challenge is in the execution. As with any skill, you must be able to do it versus just knowing about it. You can go on "practice" interviews, if you like, in order to get the feeling of the action, but it's a shame to waste any real interview situation on practice.

You might try to get a group of students together to run through some drills which will help you build skills quickly. When the standard interview questions pop up, you will feel comfortable with your preplanned response. "Where do you hope to be in five years?"

"That's a good question, and I have often asked that of myself. If I were to be in an organization like yours, what would be a reasonable answer? What were your first five years like?" Or, "In all honesty, I am working hard on the next five months, and I will have to let the five-year period develop by itself, until I get the short-term taken care of. Is that a reasonable strategy? If you were me, how would you set your objectives?"

Every answer is short, to the point, delivered politely, with a little bit of deference and almost always ending in a question. You can't just recite this. It must be delivered. It must have pauses, sincerity, thoughtfulness. If you're comfortable with yourself, the enthusiastic delivery will follow.

Every answer is short, to the point, delivered politely, with a little bit of deference and almost always ending in a question.

All of this should begin to call the whole interview process into question. And rightfully so. Interviews are not good vehicles for evaluating people and opportunities, although they at least put us face to face with a live person which is many times better than getting caught in the resume trap. Interviews are so common that you must learn to deal with them, but internships, referrals, summer jobs, the family business, or the family business of a friend are much better paths for finding your way into the action of the outside world.

> *If someone has passed you on for a second interview, he has put his judgement behind you, and it is in his best interest that you look good on the next rung.*

THE SECOND INTERVIEW

Let's say that you have survived a first evaluation interview and now must go on to seconds. You now know what the full cycle of the interview process is for this particular corporation through your questions at the initial interview. You know if there are to be third interviews. You know the proposed decision date and job start date. And, you know you have won round one, and that you now have a sponsor. Good.

If someone has passed you on for a second interview, he has put his judgement behind you, and it is in his best interest that you look good on the next rung. Before you go to your second interview, call your first interviewer on the phone, and ask what to expect in detail. Now you have a member on your team, so you can test your approach with an insider. You can ask for profiles of the people you will meet. Remember Tex? You can find out why you made it to seconds, by asking what strengths you should be building on. You can ask the exact profile of the ideal candidate, so you can emphasize those details from your background into that framework. You can set up a meeting with your sponsor to report back on results, thereby keeping the door open, and giving you some valuable feedback on how you actually were viewed during your second interview. It's now starting to get interesting.

Each stage requires its own round of correspondence. You want your follow-up notes to be professional and ever present because, just as in consumer advertising, gross rating points count. You want multiple exposures. Each follow-up note is another positive statement of your value. See why the stationery is so important? It becomes a constant statement of who you are.

If you go on to a third interview, you just repeat the process down the line. You have two friends. You can ask them for advice. It's not you against them, it's us working together.

There is no greater compliment to someone than asking for some help and advice. You must be sure to thank that person, and then act, and follow through on what was recommended. If you don't follow through, you will cut off your relationship. If someone recommends you read a specific book on advertising or management, go buy it that afternoon. Write a follow-up note when you are five chapters into it, to reinforce how valuable the book is. If your contact recommends you talk to someone else for background, copy him on your referral note, and report back as soon as you have had a meeting. It's a building block approach to data gathering. People you meet on a first or second interview at the beginning of an entry-level career search may be important to you for the rest of your life. Remember the contact treasure hunt. You can't keep in touch with everyone you meet forever, but where you detect good chemistry put yourself out a little to get back and follow through.

> *If you go on to a third interview, it's not you against them; it's us working together.*

As you move through an interview progression, it is important to overlap or work simultaneously on multiple interview chains. What you want to do is to bring several opportunities along at about the same speed. Because interviews are so much trouble to set up, the temptation is to work on one opportunity at a time. This is a poor tactic for two reasons. The very capriciousness and subjectivity of the process demands that you have multiple Plan Bs. The second factor is that by having multiple interviews or contacts going at once, you can name drop one with the other in a nice sort of way.

Knowing that you are valued by someone else greatly increases your immediate value. So the effort required to have several balls in the air at once can pay off in multiple offers and higher salary packages.

It makes little difference that you have no experience, no background, and are still a student. If you have several people interested in you, and they know about each other, your value increases way out of proportion to what you might think you have to offer. This is not just a nice add-on strategy. It is critical to the whole process. It changes the dynamics from one of straightforward evaluation to one of competetive evaluation. Suddenly, the employer has to move quickly in order not to miss picking up a resource of great value.

Having more than one ball in the air at all times makes them all go higher. If you drop some, there are still others up there. Plus having several developing opportunities at once changes your approach. You begin feeling confident (not overconfident), your interview skills get sharper, and you are in top form from the excitement of the whole process. This positive energy translates to good vibes all around.

There is no end to the action you can create, if you just understand that self-promotion feeds on itself. Within

> *Having more than one ball in the air at all times makes them all go higher.*

> *Being somebody of value is one thing. Being perceived as someone of value is another.*

> **Good questions are like reusable silver bullets. Once you have them, it just requires timing and marksmanship in order to score points.**

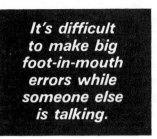

reasonable bounds, it can go on indefinitely. Being somebody of value is one thing. Being perceived as someone of value is another. Hopefully you can be both, but given the choice between the two, take the perception and the substance will follow. The reverse is not always true.

After each interview encounter, after the notes have been written and the follow-up action planned, sit down and say to yourself, "What went right? What worked? How close did I come to my preinterview objective? How appropriate was the objective?"

Identify all of the positives of the experience, all of the good questions, all of the little turnarounds, all of the pluses. These are the elements you want to reinforce. These are the things you want to be able to do again when the situation dictates. When they said this . . . I said that . . . Wow!, and . . . it worked. Good questions are like reusable silver bullets. Once you have them, it just requires timing and marksmanship in order to score points.

There are thousands of things you can do wrong in an interview. Don't worry about them. Figure out what you can do right. Asking questions always puts the ball in the other court.

It's difficult to make big foot-in-mouth errors while someone else is talking. Working from a plan and a written list of questions will become more natural as you do it more often. One student commented, after accepting a job, that it was almost a shame to do so, because he was getting so good at the interview process.

The process never ends. Keep the skills polished. But, first, you must create them. Whether it's a student's informational interview, a candidate's first "white socks" interview, a second interview pass-along, a third interview for a higher-up blessing, or a fourth interview for an offer, all of the same skills apply. Clarify your objectives (another meeting—not a job . . . . yet), develop a written list of questions, keep your answers short. Keep the ball in the other court. Get them to like you first as a person and second as a potential professional. Do it all with good questions. And now, go to it.

CHAPTER 9

BIG
NAME
OR BIG
OPPORTUNITY?

> **Many so-called training programs just delay your opportunity to begin doing meaningful work. You need a track to run on not a cart to ride around it in.**

> **The illusion that is created by selectivity is that those selected are destined for greatness. All that really happens is that the opportunities get fewer and fewer as you move along, and the price you must pay gets higher and higher.**

Y ou have been in school for most of your life. The time has now come to begin doing, to begin contributing, to begin achieving results. Whatever you do will be a learning experience. That's a given. Your development from here on in will be an evolution of self . . . yourself. Avoid postponing this experiential phase of growing. Avoid training programs. Many so-called training programs just delay your opportunity to begin doing meaningful work. You need a track to run on not a cart to ride around it in. Have the confidence to go give it your best shot. The returns are there for the taking. Whenever you start to narrow your options, ask yourself, "What are the returns to me in both income and saleable experience? How much time must I invest to get a return?"

There is a great deal of standard wisdom on where best to begin a career. Much of this discussion has merit, but its absolute value is marginal at best. Before you come up with an ironclad set of procedures and qualifications for launching your career, consider the advantages of the full range of possibilities.

BIG CORPORATE STRATEGY

One major company used its field sales force as a vehicle for developing management talent. There are few better places to learn a business than face to face with customers. In this company, eight- or nine-months time in a junior position usually resulted in promotion, and on occasion, relocation to a full sales territory. Eighteen-months to two-years later a major market or senior territory provided the ultimate test. A year in the major market and the candidate was then considered for a first step into management. That job also required a relocation and reported to a senior regional manager. The duties now involved recruiting and training sales people in one quarter of the United States. This required up to a 90 percent travel schedule.

Few people were kept in that job for over a year, because they were then promoted to a senior district where they became assistant managers. Two years later, when a job opened up, the assistant manager was made district manager in a small district of his own. If you have been counting the years and the moves, you know it could be as many as nine years with four or five moves.

When the employees completed this program, they were well-versed in both the overall business and in first-line management. Their income was low to moderate by most standards, but they had the assurance that they were among an elite few who had passed the test of fire in a major multi-national company. One or two individuals passed on to staff positions, and every four or five years a regional manager made it to Vice-President of Sales for a division. The payoff, if you can call it that, came in the mid-fifty age bracket in the form of a career regional manager's slot; every ten years or so, someone was rewarded with an international assignment.

The picture to keep in mind when looking at this kind of process is one of an inverted funnel. Even though the entry area is wide, it is still very selective, because of the visibility and name recognition value of the big company. The illusion that is created by selectivity is that those selected are destined for greatness. All that really happens is that the opportunities get fewer and fewer as you move along, and the price you must pay gets higher and higher. The payout is far over the horizon and the

> **The logic for you, if you go with the big company, is to pick an outpoint and hang on to it.**

odds of getting to it are astronomical. If you do have the luck, fortitude, and ability to win at this type of game, then you most likely could win bigger and far sooner in many lesser, but more rewarding, companies.

The logic for you, if you go with the big company, is to pick an outpoint and hang on to it. You want to take their image and name, add it to your own, then take the combination back into the marketplace and see what you can get for it. Sounds easy, but when you are flown to the home office with your spouse on the corporate jet for dinner with the top management, it is difficult to be cold and calculating. It's far easier to see yourself on the other side of one of those big desks, if you are willing to continue to pay the price. Myth number one about joining large corporations, then, is that you are destined for greatness.

The career problems in the big company strategy surface between eight and fifteen years in (if you can project yourself that far), so they are not of immediate concern. Actually, most people, either by their choice or circumstances, work their way out of a big company within the first eighteeen to twenty four months, so not to worry, but be aware.

> **Big companies promote the idea of full career employment. They sell what is sometimes known as the big promise.**

Big companies promote the idea of full career employment. They sell what is sometimes known as the big promise. Those who are in big companies have obviously committed themselves to the corporate life-style, so they tend to try to make a good case for it (if for no other reason than to reassure themselves).

There is an unjustified illusion of security inside the walls of the big company. Their newsletters list those getting their thirty-five year pins, and the gate guards have been there forever. In fact, considerable turnover takes place, and often it is involuntary. At any point in your career, you can run across a superior who doesn't think much of you for whatever reason, and in ninety days, you can be on the outside looking in.

Divisions are bought and sold, business cycles shift, all kinds of things cause ebbs and flows, so the long-term "security" of the big company is myth number two. Understanding these myths and images should help you to interview well with a big company, because they look for people who fit the long-term myth.

Asking about long-term goals and extended career paths usually gets big company people going in glowing terms. They almost always tell the story of the current president or chairman of the board who thirty years ago started in this very same management development program. You, of course, know that three hundred others were washed out along the way in order to make one success story, but interjecting that reality is not appropriate.

The best thing the big company has going for it is name recognition. If you sign on with them, you then get the name to put behind yours. Even if you only stay a year or two you can always say, "Oh, yes, I was with GM,

> There is an unjustified illusion of security inside the walls of the big company.

> The best thing the big company has going for it is name recognition. If you sign on with them, you then get the name to put behind yours.

Don't get carried away. Many long-term big company employees are more inmates than anything else. Understand where the value is.

Try not to be stampeded or panicked by the name game. If you need one and want to pay the price, go get yourself one, but be sure you understand what you are getting.

AT & T, Bank of America" or whatever. You can say that for your entire career, so big company name recognition has real value. But don't get carried away. Many long-term big company employees are more inmates than anything else. Understand where the value is.

There is also a big company name game that you should be aware of. Many college seniors will attempt to interview with and get offers from as many name organizations as possible. What they are doing is trying to reinforce their own identities with the image of a corporate giant. It's a need motivated by a little insecurity, and has nothing to do with the real work of making a solid entry-level contact with a person who will help you get started. Because everyone in the last year or two of college is in transition, it becomes a subject of general conversation and having some big names to talk about provides a measure of social security.

This process extends to parents who like to be able to say, "Oh, yes, she will be going with United Technologies when she graduates. Had six big offers. Turned down Exxon, Citicorp, and one or two others. U.T. is a great organization, you know."

Try not to be stampeded or panicked by the name game. If you need one and want to pay the price, go get yourself one, but be sure you understand what you are getting.

THE SMALL ORGANIZATION

If not a name, what about opportunity? Isn't that what small organizations have to offer? Yes, they do, but again at a price. The small company tries to get people at a low price with the promise of great things to come. You can be assured of being busy from day one with a small company, because it is almost always a learn-as-you-go situation.

If you report directly to someone who knows what he or she is doing, and who will take the time to housebreak you, that's an almost ideal situation. And, it won't take two years to get into the flow of an operation. In six months, it is amazing how knowledgeable and even valuable you can become. The small company is usually short on budgets, and big on creativity. You can try things, if they don't cost very much.

Results are what count and small businesses are highly number sensitive. Again, if you get a chance at working face to face with customers and can have an influence on income in any way, you will have a chance to make a name for yourself much sooner than you might think. Although there is some dues paying, the action tends to pick up pretty fast in small or growing outfits.

The goals of gaining experience and learning are valid, but that can only be a secondary objective. Contributing, doing something, accomplishing a goal must be primary. You want a chance to be a part of the action and to make a difference. A small difference, perhaps at first, but a difference nonetheless.

You have had your "training." It's now time for doing. Don't worry. You will not be asked to split the stock or make a major scientific breakthrough in your first six months, but you will be asked to help out and add your presence to the effort.

Don't look for formal structure in the small organization. It's the informal information and unwritten rules and principles that are important. You need someone to explain to you what is going on. That is why it is vital that you get a good solid first manager. You need someone who is not so busy with what he is doing that he can't take time to answer a multitude of entry-level questions.

One small outfit added its first junior level staff person. Each day the president, vice-president, and the comptroller took the wet-behind-the-ears graduate to lunch with them to the nearby sandwich shop. The conversation ranged across the aging of receivables, to new product development, to the selection of a new plant site.

Each evening, when the clerical staff went home, the management gathered in the president's office and talked over what was going on. These little seminars covered every area of the growth of this company. Just the dynamics of how the management team interacted was an extended lesson in the operation of power.

Three years of this afterhours development made a solid contributor out of our junior manager. There were no simulations. Everything was real. When a big company assignment became available later, he discovered that all of the principles of operation and management which he had learned in the little company, applied perfectly in the giant organization.

It took the big company longer and they spent more money, but they did the same things. There were no complex formulas. There were no sophisticated models. It was all there in the big international giant, just the way it had been in the little operation. Managing people was the same, budget work was identical except for the extra sets of zeros on all reports. It all fit. So either way, you will address the same challenges with the same techniques. You get at them much sooner in the little organization, but they will all be there. With thousands of employees you would think that movement in a big company would be much easier; in fact, interdepartmental and interdisciplinary moves in big companies are discouraged. They try to stabilize the operation as much as possible. In essence, they become

> **With thousands of employees you would think that movement in a big company would be much easier; in fact, interdepartmental and interdisciplinary moves in big companies are discouraged.**

groupings of little organizations. In small companies, you have to contend with the owners, and often their families as well. Those are just facts of life and nothing is forever.

> **If you think in terms of eighteen-month opportunities instead of eighteen-year careers, you will be in a much more realistic mind-set.**

> **At one time or another in a career, it would be nice to have both big and little exposure.**

NOT A MARRIAGE, JUST A JOB

If you think in terms of eighteen-month opportunities instead of eighteen-year careers, you will be in a much more realistic mind set. It is highly unlikely that you will stay with a first job forever, so don't make plans in that direction (except during interviews). The big company is not essential for your first career move, nor is it necessary to go with a small group so busy with survival that you lack the attention required for a good start.

At one time or another in a career, it would be nice to have both big and little exposure. It doesn't make much difference when you get it, or even if you get it, so it's hard to make an error except by being overly selective or dogmatic in your entry-level strategy. Several quick moves with small-or medium-size organizations can run your salary scale up rapidly. Then you can sell that experience to a name outfit at a price that would have taken many years to achieve coming up through their ranks.

Although college was a four-year undertaking (and sometimes five or six), there is no need to make plans for an extended tour with any one organization. The eighteen-month time-frame is a good one for planning purposes. That means in twelve months you will evaluate the situation based on what you have learned up to that point. If a move is indicated, you will have a year's experience plus a six-month period to set up your movement strategy.

This short-term view must be your personal view, because those who do the hiring (both big and small) think in terms of extended or even lifelong commitments. Let them think that way just so long as you don't start making decisions based on these unrealistic extended time-frames.

Your job now is to talk to large numbers of potential employers, both big and small. Tell the big outfits that you have some entrepreneurial opportunities which make you look like a valued, creative self-starter. Tell the small companies that you are dealing with the biggies, so that you seem to be of national value. Naming and talking about your alternatives in a matter of fact way, as well as posing some, "What would you do if you were me?" questions are excellent tactics.

If, all of a sudden, it is beginning to become apparent that this sounds like a lot of horse trading with you being the horse, you are right.

Many people dislike negotiations or the lack of stability in maneuvering. They are anxious to get started in a job, any job. Don't be in too great a hurry. The selection process on both sides is a very valuable developmental experience and should not be rushed. Patience and the ability to work the process will pay off both short term with the best possible deal, as well as long term with the added confidence to enable you to work the system in the future. (And then there are those lifeboat contacts.)

> **If, all of a sudden, it is beginning to become apparent that this sounds like a lot of horse trading with you being the horse, you are right.**

> **A flexible strategy that keeps as many options open for as long as possible seems to be about the best.**

> **So, the plot begins to thicken. It's not one job, but two jobs that are the objective.**

If, of course, from an informational interview you were able to get an internship that resulted in a full-time offer and the vibes were good, go right ahead and take it. You can pick up all your maneuvering experience on the first bounce a year down the road.

A flexible strategy that keeps as many options open for as long as possible seems to be about the best. Chances to look over large numbers of opportunities, rather than one or two potential sure things, is the ideal. Try not to sell yourself short by going for the first shot that shows, unless it's a really good one. As rough, raw material, you are of considerable value to many, many organizations. Remember they are trying to close a sale with you as soon as they decide on your value. When the ball shifts to the other court, be ready.

Keep Plan B viable, in case something goes wrong. It's always a good idea to take your selection process down to at least two or even three finalists. Keep in mind you are selecting. That means regardless of your first choice, you should follow through with second and third best all the way through to the offer stage. I know it's a great deal of trouble to do this when you know who your first choice is, and you just about have the job, but it can save all kinds of trouble in return for the extra effort.

Quick terminations are more likely in smaller than in larger organizations, but a Plan B lifeboat will be of value at all times.

So, the plot begins to thicken. It's not one job, but two jobs that are the objective. It's not just a name organization to impress your friends, but rather a one-on-one personal commitment between you and whomever

It's not a training program you need, but a chance to contribute.

you will be working for directly. It's not a training program you need, but a chance to contribute. You will learn no matter where you go. It's not a career path you need, it's a start. If someone wants to sell you a career, be careful you don't pay too much for it.

Although it may not sound very scientific, or even businesslike, where you feel warmest and most comfortable will most likely be the best place for your first job.

Everything else you can add on as you go along. Knowing it's hard to go wrong should encourage you to begin moving in many directions. Open all the doors. There is no telling what will be behind them.

CHAPTER **10**

HEADHUNTERS,

FLESHPEDDLERS,

BODYSNATCHERS,

& THE CLASSIFIED:

WHAT THEY

ARE ALL

ABOUT

> # The people placement business works just like any other business; it must serve a customer in order to get paid.

There seems to be a feeling that a great and powerful personnel industry services our economy and one need merely place his or her body in the breach of this giant engine to be catapulted into the land of opportunity.

As with many of the points in this book, there is some truth to the story, but how it actually works is a world of difference from how it is normally perceived.

The people placement business works just like any other business; it must serve a customer in order to get paid. The customer or client in this case is the organization, company, or business that needs talent and is willing to pay someone to find that talent for it. Putting yourself on the other side of the desk for a moment or two, ask yourself why you would pay good money for this kind of service, when an ad in the paper will draw all kinds of resumes in response.

The answer is that you want a specific type of person and for that type you will pay 30 percent of the first year salary to a placement firm. In order to justify that cost, you need a supplier who will provide a profile match of experience and industry background, so that the new employee will begin to contribute to your operation almost at once. The concept of background and experience translating into future performance is not totally valid, but for a busy manager it appears to be a reasonable shortcut and definitely worth paying for. You have only to sit in an office for two or three days, screening applicants, to understand the need for someone to do this for you.

So, the personnel industry—and we will talk about all of its elements shortly—first must provide basic screening services, and second, is charged with coming up with hard-to-find profile matches that fit whatever requirements and specifications have been established by the client.

Stop and think for a minute how an entry-level/recent college graduate fits into this process. The answer is that first job-seekers don't fit. An applicant with little specific experience is a difficult, if not impossible, product for a service firm to market profitably. Obviously, inexperienced applicants are seeking entry-level positions, so the salaries they command and their related fee percentage for the placement organization can't justify a marketing effort. Plus the inexperienced applicant won't have the background experience to be marketable for that perfect match.

So for better or for worse, the placement industry generally is set up to function on a level one or two pegs above where college graduates will enter the marketplace.

This makes the entry process almost exclusively a do-it-yourself type project. There are some minor exceptions to this rule, particularly if you have trade school concentration or some discipline which may be initially marketable. The chances of that are rare. There is little need to go out and visit with the professional placement people.

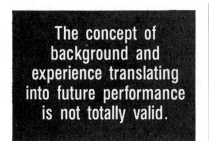

The concept of background and experience translating into future performance is not totally valid.

> **There are jobs in the newspaper classifieds; it's just that, with only a few exceptions, they are the wrong kinds of jobs.**

WHAT ABOUT THE CLASSIFIEDS?

The one area that seems tailor-made for the entry-level person is the newspaper classified ads. That has to be where the jobs are! Yes, there are jobs in the newspaper classifieds; it's just that, with only a few exceptions, they are the wrong kinds of jobs.

It is estimated that only about 10 percent of jobs are advertised. Why is that? First of all, advertising is not cheap, and it carries with it the secondary costs of screening responses. It doesn't take long to discover that job advertising produces low to marginal return on the investment. The applicant pool responding to ads is all over the lot. Many people who respond to ads do not have a clear idea of what the job requirements are, nor do they have a realistic view of themselves. The result is a high level of frustration on both sides.

Blind ads, which do not name the advertiser but merely list a box number for reply, are even more frustrating. The position descriptions in these ads by definition tell even less than those run by companies that identify themselves, and the result is even more speculative responses.

In the midst of this morass, there are jobs. The capricious nature of this route to the marketplace provides its own unique challenges. The best use of classified ads is as an overall indicator of what is going on, and what specific qualifications are listed as being desirable for which jobs in which industries. It is also good to know which companies are hiring and, therefore, are likely to be growing, making them logical candidates for contact approaches.

So, the reading of the classifieds for general rather than specific information is not a bad idea. First look over the named advertisers. Check the types of opportunities they have and at what locations. This will tell you what is being done where.

Last, but not least, read the blind ads for qualifications. See what is being asked for. This will give you some clues as to the disciplines that are in demand. Even though the ads may be for senior-level people, they could indicate junior-level unadvertised demand.

Once you have been through the full classified section, go back and pick out those ads you might like to respond to if you feel compelled to participate in this arbitrary process. Your objective, remember, is not to get a job, but to avoid being screened out. It's just about impossible to figure out a winning strategy. There are no rules or formulas because the screen-out process is so subjective, and you have no idea who is doing the screening.

You must be satisfied with an attempt at a nonlosing response. You want to provide just enough information to raise interest, but not enough to be eliminated. It is best to try to err on the side of too little data rather than too much. It is better to be conservative rather than distinctive.

If this sounds like a crap shoot, you are right. That's not to say you shouldn't answer classified ads, but it can't be your primary strategy, unless you want to develop a particularly thick skin and remain in the ad-answering business for an extended period of your life.

Many ads will say send resume and salary requirements. If you decide to respond at all, at least give yourself as good a chance as the circumstances allow. Write an ad-specific resume, around what the ad requires. List your objectives in the specific terms of the ad. Tie in whatever background you have to the elements listed in the discription of the position. Do not list elements that do not directly apply. Don't volunteer extra information. Don't try for long shots in matching experience. Provide as little data as possible in as standard a form as possible. Keep everything clean and simple. Request an informational meeting. Be sure your name, address, and telephone number are on both your cover letter and resume. Specify a calling time. (Telephone screeners often just skip over no-answer responses.)

Be prepared for a telephone contact. Have a list of written questions. Ask for a face-to-face meeting. Don't be discouraged if your best efforts get absolutely no response at all, or if what appears to you to be the ideal fit is screened out with a couple of telephone questions. As far as salary requirements are concerned, always talk in terms of ranges, i.e. mid-twenties, low-thirties, six figure, etc. You can pick up ranges from other similar ads. It's also not difficult to develop salary ranges from informational interviews, industry contacts, internships or whatever first-hand source you can get in touch with. So long as you do not ask someone's specific income, a source will normally give you the range in the industry or organization. Once you have that data, your response to salary requirements should be set at a median level, so as not to cause screen-out. Salary negotiations come far down the list; it is not a good idea to lead with your chin on an initial response. Keep in mind the objective of arranging a meeting. That objective is different from landing a job; you must constantly think in terms of one and not the other.

A CLOSE-UP OF AD RESPONSES

Here's one specific example that actually happened, and in many respects is all too typical. The numbers cited are not exaggerated.

A job vacancy developed because of a resignation in a major southeastern city. The position could be filled by either an entry-level person or someone with industry experience. The regional manager asked for a little help in the recruiting and selection from a home-office staff person. They planned to meet in the field and screen applicants.

On the Sunday prior to the scheduled Wednesday meeting, the staff person ran an ad in the local paper listing the job and the name of the national company involved. He also listed his own name for a reply and gave the address of the hotel he was to use for interviewing as the response location. On Tuesday afternoon, he arrived from the airport to check in and was given a warm welcome by the registration desk personnel. They all wanted to see this very important person because calls had been coming in since Sunday afternoon, and the amount of mail was now overflowing two cardboard boxes.

Adding the boxes to his luggage, he had them all trucked up to his suite. A quick count brought the number of replies to over three hundred.

Economic times were not particularly bad and unemployent in the area was normal. The big company name was the draw. Almost one hundred of the responses had no postage on them indicating that they were hand-delivered.

It took two hours after dinner for a quick sort, just to get a flavor for what was in the piles. That turned up two veteran employees of competing companies who obviously would know the business in the area. At least a dozen minority applicants were apparent from names and educational backgrounds. It was after midnight by the time everything was read through once; this first screening produced twenty-five potential interviewees. The following morning when the local manager arrived, he was happy to see all the work that had been done. He took charge of the two boxes of rejects who would get form letters in reply. Companies of this size have images to maintain so replies are mandatory. By nine A.M., the phone began to ring. About twenty calls came in from local employment agencies that wanted to send over candidates and were trying to get an agreement on a contingency fee. Because the talent pool was more than adequate, the two company men decided to stick with the responses they had. Twenty-five more responses came with the Wednesday morning mail. They produced one additional prime candidate.

Telephone interviews rounded off the number of people actually to be seen to ten. Whenever the phone was put down, it rang with either another agency call or one of the applicants following up on a resume.

On Thursday, the ten candidates were interviewed, with six of them being screened out in forty-five minute interviews. Another eighteen resumes arrived, were looked over as best possible, and put into the reject boxes.

Of the four finalists, two were actually hired—one of the veterans from the competition with six years experience in that market, and an entry-level minority person as a trainee. This made a good two-person team.

When the interview team departed on Friday, resumes were still coming in. They ended up sending over four hundred reject form letters.

One of the two people hired stayed three years; the other left after fourteen months. The recruiting job was done again at that time by another management team.

STEER CLEAR OF
CAREER-COUNSELING FIRMS

Career-counseling firms are very careful to point out that they are not employment agencies, but offer career services only. They will prepare resumes, give the applicant professional evaluations, videotape interview training, and provide access to computer databanks of potential employers. On the surface, this sounds like a valuable service, especially for someone who is not experienced in the marketplace. These operations are questionable at best. They begin with selling the applicant a service contract. Throughout the contract the statement is constantly made that no results are guaranteed. The catch is that all the services under contract seem to be directly related to job placement. They're not.

As a student you shouldn't be afraid to present yourself as exactly what you are.

PROFESSIONAL PLACEMENT FIRMS

Because the professional placement industry is very alluring and active, and because you really should avoid wasting your time and money at this point, you need to know just how it works and all its variations. This is strictly for information because you are much better off on your own. Here is how the hierarchy is arranged.

At the top of the pyramid are executive search firms or search consultants. Many of these companies are national in scope. A classic search assignment is done on an exclusive retainer basis; it is rather expensive, and it is used only for high-level positions. The consultant is paid whether the client hires anyone or not.

Almost every organization in the industry says it does search work, because that indicates a high level of professionalism. In most cases, these organizations do little if any retainer search work.

Because true executive search assignments are rare, other types of services must be done for clients in order to provide a sound business mix. Occasionally, a search consultant will take on an assignment to help fill a lower-level or middle-management need. This is done on a billable hour basis. In these cases, usually a specific discipline with industry background is needed. A financial executive with consumer goods experience is how these needs are expressed. If the consultant has contacts in the consumer goods field, he will call and see if anyone fits the assignment.

All of this is still well above anything that a recent graduate would become involved in. Dealing with search firms can be learned at a later date, if appropriate. All you have to know now is that they exist, but not for students. The essence of the search business is finding big business clients, not candidates, at any rate. So much for background.

FLESH PEDDLERS/ PLACEMENT FIRMS

A little closer to home would be those firms that specialize in lower-level positions, made profitable by working on volume. They often operate on a contingency basis, meaning they get paid if they create a match. The actual placement people are commission sales representatives and they do a great deal of telephone sales contact work. They try to locate middle managers who hire in high-turnover jobs; then the reps sell applicants who fit the profiles of the industry in question. They average five completed telephone calls (not sales) for every fifty calls made. Not a fun business.

These firms sometimes just shift people from one company to another at about the same salary levels. To get into these "paper mills," so called because they bombard potential clients with hundreds of spec-sheet type resumes, all an applicant needs is about a year's industry-specific experience. You then become marketable through this channel of distribution. These types of operations are the originators of the term "flesh peddlers." The sales representative, euphemistically called a counselor, is paid from the business client's fees and, therefore, as a broker, has the client's (not the applicant's) best interest—or more likely his or her own commission—as a first priority. Steer clear.

As a student you shouldn't be afraid to present yourself as exactly what you are. You are a potential entry-level employee who wants to contribute to the success of an organization. That is a most useful position to be in. Almost everyone can identify with your situation. Everyone knows you must begin at sometime and at someplace, so don't worry about all the ads and agencies that are looking for exotic experience profiles. All they indicate is that there is action out there somewhere. Use them as pieces of your treasure-hunt map. Gather the data and apply it positively.

Always be aware of how the contact-referral process works, as that's your main avenue of pursuit. Then, if an occasional alternative that fits your situation (such as an ad specifying entry level or an agency which is trying to hire a large number of new graduates for a specific assignment) comes along, by all means, pursue the lead.

Let the applicant beware. You can waste a great deal of time, effort, and frustration thinking that someone will discover you in a pile of applications and resumes, or that some "counselor" will find you a position.

Knowing how all the placement and employment people function will save you the time and frustration of trying to fit yourself into a system that was not designed to be of primary use to you.

Let the applicant beware. You can waste a great deal of time, effort, and frustration thinking that someone will discover you in a pile of applications and resumes, or that some "counselor" will find you a position. In the case of a job search, doing it yourself is the only way to assure a quality result. After you get through the entry level, you can then take a look at the placement industry, working it selectively for future moves along with your never-ending contact chain.

You should now begin to see some of the reasons why personal contact marketing approaches have validity. Sooner or later you must accept the situation as it is and do all the work required. There is no outside organized help of any value, so get organized yourself. It isn't difficult; all of the steps described so far surely can be done. The catch is you have to do them.

There are all kinds of innovative people coming up with ideas to get around the chaos of the job market. There are video cassette resumes, computer databanks for member organizations, job fairs, open houses, and any number of other approaches to solving the dilemma of getting people who may be of help to one another together.

> **The fact that you are a unique, highly adaptable, human being makes it difficult to fit into standard screening systems.**

The fact that you are a unique, highly adaptable, flexible human being makes it difficult to fit into standard screening systems. Trying to fit into the system will more often result in getting lost in the system, or at the very least, getting discounted by the system.

By concentrating your efforts on unique one-on-one personal contacts, you increase your chances of a fair evaluation or positive encounter many, many times over.

CHAPTER 11

OFFERS:
SOONER
OR LATER
YOU WILL
GET SOME

*Keep in mind
that the primary
objective of your
job search or
campaign is not
a job, but the
generation of offers.*

*Offers are
like rabbits; one
is nice but two make
for many, many more.*

*Evaluating jobs
before you have
offers is a
waste of time.
There is nothing
to evaluate.*

Keep in mind that the primary objective of your job search or campaign is not a job, but the generation of offers.

Overlooking this intermediate goal causes your efforts to be misfocused. By thinking in terms of offers and how to get them, you are much more likely to be able to generate a group of them, rather than just a single response. Offers are like rabbits; one is nice but two make for many, many more. To come up with the best offer requires a bunch. One offer at a time eliminates the multiplier effect.

Evaluating jobs before you have offers is a waste of time. There is nothing to evaluate. Only when you have firm offers in writing can you begin the real work of deciding what's best for you at this point in your life. An offer is not a job. It is an invitation to come to work at a specific position. Getting an invite and being able to do a job are two separate things. Don't mix them up. Focus

> *Focus only on those things that will produce offers. Forget the job. That comes later.*

only on those things that will produce offers. Forget the job. That comes later.

It's a natural temptation to project yourself into a job from almost the very first contact. That projection gets in the way of pressing home your efforts for a viable offer.

The business of getting a job is a two-sided selling situation. It's not in your best interest to allow it to become a one-way selection process. You have to keep reminding yourself how valuable you are. Having several offers builds the value image for both you and your prospective employers. That value image changes the dynamics of the process.

The importance of generating multiple offers can't be stressed enough. They feed off one another. Some can be put on ice. Some can be held up for months or even years, if they are handled correctly. They can be tremendously valuable career insurance policies.

One marketing type managed to get two offers at just about the same time from two first class companies. Accepting the best deal was not the problem. Getting the losing outfit to accept the loss in such a way that it could be kept as a future contact was the challenge. Our candidate made an extra visit to the rejected company, touched all the bases, and left a solid feeling behind. The casual parting comment of "if things don't work out, be sure to get back to us" was the objective he wished to achieve. Within six months, things did not work out. The position accepted wasn't as promised. The budgets were not there. The support was lacking. In spite of the exercise of the best possible judgement, the job began to come apart. A single phone call reactivated the backup offer in spite of the elapsed time. He made the move. It worked out well for all concerned. If the shoe had been on the other foot and the first company had not liked his performance, it would have had no qualms about firing the manager. As it was, he had no qualms about leaving.

> *If you take a company to the offer stage, you then have passed the test and are considered a viable prospect. If you pull out before that final stage, you are just a screened-out candidate.*

In this case, the carefully managed multiple offers proved to be a lifeboat system that had to be used much sooner than expected.

If you take a company to the offer stage, you then have passed the test and are considered a viable prospect. If you pull out before that final stage, you are just a screened-out candidate. Offers are like passports for future visits. Always press home the last step even if you are certain you will be going elsewhere. Just the experience of closing the deal makes it well worth the extra effort.

If you turn down an offer leaving the impression that "we almost had him or her," you leave the company with a warm feeling about you. There is nothing wrong with keeping that feeling alive with key decision-makers over a long period of time. For one thing, some of those key people may leave for other opportunities, thereby doubling the number of places where you might be welcome. All this is possible, if you will just go the extra mile to generate a valid offer. It's not unfair to take these steps even though you think you have your first choice in the bag. It's good business for all concerned. The fact that your prospects are aware that you have multiple

> *The fact that your prospects are aware that you have multiple offers always increases your value.*

offers always increases your value. It may or may not increase starting salaries or benefits, but that is not the objective. Becoming a more valued acquisition is good enough for now.

GENERATING OFFERS

If offers are your objective, how are they generated? That's a good question and one you should ask on a first or second interview, during an internship, an informational series of contacts, or when a potential opening is identified.

You may be talking to a junior person at that point, so there will be no decision pressure applied. It will just be a normal information request and that's when you want to garner this valuable data for later use. How are offers made in this organization? Who do they come from? What is the chain of approval? You may find out that a personnel requisition must be generated or that salary budgets must be adjusted. Knowing this gives you a nice directional question to ask when you get to the point in the process where you want to generate some action. Determining who signs a written offer also will be of value, so you can avoid trying to close with the wrong person. Asking about the normal time sequence involved will give you lead time to work on other prospects. Gathering offer data and procedures early in the process sends a message that you are a serious candidate.

As a student you have the advantage of being able to go for an offer as much as a year in advance of actually taking a job. Many companies will extend an offer at the end of a junior year summer internship. Some students then take that as a license for a delightful senior year. The wise move is to take the one offer in hand, and then begin to see how many more can be generated to provide perspective, or as mentioned, for lifeboat and future contact.

The earlier you get offers the better, but don't panic. You are asking an organization to make a major commitment and expenditure. One of the best business practices there is requires extended hiring and evaluation periods. It is normal for this process to go on for several months. Take advantage of this time lag to go for three

> *Don't rush it.*
> *Even if you are*
> *about to graduate*
> *and are the lost*
> *soul with no*
> *place to go, you*
> *still must work*
> *the system and*
> *operate on*
> *someone else's*
> *time priorities.*

> *The pace belongs*
> *to them not to you,*
> *so the best you can*
> *do is to get*
> *several games going*
> *at once. Play them*
> *all for real no*
> *matter what your*
> *preferences may be.*

or four potential offers. Don't rush it. Even if you are about to graduate and are the lost soul with no place to go, you still must work the system and operate on someone else's time priorities. If you graduate without an offer, that just means you will be able to work full time on generating live ones without distractions. It's in everyone's best interest to proceed slowly, so don't feel that you are unwanted and unloved just because of a three-or four-month decision period.

One candidate went through a six-month process during which no one said "no" and everyone thought "he would be just right." It took that long to coordinate travel schedules and approvals, so everyone would be in sinc when he finally came on board. A year or two later when going through files he discovered that the company had been looking for an applicant like him for two years before he had ever made contact. Why did it take so long? They had a system of operation that happened to be very deliberate. The pace belongs to them not to you, so the best you can do is to get several games going at once. Play them all for real no matter what your preferences may be. You have no options until you have actual written offers.

Once you have learned the time sequence, plus who the key decision maker is, then it is acceptable, and in fact considered to be good form, to go for the close and ask for an offer. At entry level, there are few points that are negotiable, but some do come up. You can find out in advance what the salary range is, and also when the first review period is scheduled. Many companies have a six-month review period for a new hire, so your salary may actually be considerably greater at the end of the first year.

If there are special situations you would like to negotiate, the time to do it is after the offer is made. You can't ask to have policies changed just for you, but if a company has made a written offer, it has indicated it wants you and little add-ons or slight changes for the sake of convenience can often be gained without difficulty. Some offers will run several pages and many factors can be made a part of the deal.

A company car is no small thing; if a great deal of highway travel is involved, an upgrade to a heavier, more road-worthy car can be a swing item. Cars are often chosen for the whole company by those in the accounting department who seldom ride in them. If you take a road assignment, your car can be a major factor in your overall well-being. Taking what's available may be the only option, but if a new car must be purchased, you might as well state your preference, if you feel it is appropriate. How will you know if it's appropriate? Again, by asking others earlier in the process, you can form a judgement that will give you an idea of what can and can't be done.

It is company policy in some firms not to negotiate starting salaries, but they often have "sign-up bonus funds" available. A few thousand extra dollars up front will be ample compensation for your having carried several other prospects to the offer stage. See how your value image works? If you appear to be in demand, that might justify a sign-up bonus.

> *If there are special situations you would like to negotiate, the time to do it is after the offer is made.*

You can't take offers one at a time. They all must be working at once to produce positive multiplier effects. I can't hammer this point home enough. You can use the experience gained in one offer negotiation to great benefit with other companies or organizations. Putting all of your eggs in one basket will just assure a lot of broken eggs, if the basket is dropped. You want a lot of baskets and a lot of eggs. Don't worry about the uncertainty. That's not your concern. The multiple-offer dynamics are what you are trying to generate.

Putting all of your eggs in one basket will just assure a lot of broken eggs, if the basket is dropped. You want a lot of baskets and a lot of eggs.

Because of the subjective nature of the selection process, it is very possible to do everything right and not get an offer.

Because of the subjective nature of the selection process, it is very possible to do everything right and not get an offer. How do you know the status of the budget, or the executive in a particular function, and what he can and can't do? You don't. How do you know that the last three people hired from your school or part of the country didn't work out? You don't. I know that has nothing to do with what you can do, but the nature of how people select others defies reason.

Even when it looks like smooth sailing, get a bunch of offers or potential offers going all at once. Going for offers (not jobs) in companies that are way down on your list is an excellent learning process, and every so often, you will be surprised by the high quality of the opportunity.

> *If one factor can be considered the most important in evaluating an offer, it is by far your perceived potential relationship with the person you will be reporting to.*

WHEN YOU GET A LIVE ONE

Some offers will not stay on ice. Once a company decides it wants you, those in charge are smart enough to know that it is in their best interest to press you for a decision. There is no inconsistency in jerking you around for three months, and then asking you for a response in three days. They will sometimes make a verbal offer which gives you the time to ask for a written offer or letter. Once you get the written offer, you can then ask to visit one more time with your immediate superior. This visit is important because you can ask in detail for the objectives of both your job and theirs for the next six-to twelve-month period.

This brings up the point of whom you will work for. There are times when you will take a job with a big organization without having a direct report assigned to you. This is sometimes common during initial training and orientation of recent college graduates. It's a very poor practice on both sides, and should be avoided if at all possible.

If one factor can be considered the most important in evaluating an offer, it is by far your perceived potential relationship with the person you will be reporting to. Do your best to carefully evaluate your superior, because this person will become a major factor in your life. Talking with others who work for him, or have worked for him, will give you some leads. If, for example, a sales job is in the works, be sure to go out in the field and work with people in the unit you will be joining. Finding out how they have been treated by the boss is a legitimate point for research on your part. No one is going to hang out the dirty laundry for you, but a lack of rave reviews will tell you something.

Beware of going to work for a workaholic. If your boss gets to the office at seven A.M. and is still there at seven P.M., avoid him like the plague. Workaholics delegate nothing. They are self-reliant and are notorious for holding back key bits of information from subordinates in order to create artificial dependence. A fast-paced manager will give you little of the time, feedback, and guidance you will need to come up to speed. Be very, very careful to whom you commit yourself and your career.

It's not that things won't change; in fact, they often do and even a solid evaluation of your future boss may prove futile if he or she is promoted six months after you sign on. Even that can be detected in the offer evaluation process, because you will track your future boss's career path during the interview process. If your boss has had a new assignment every eighteen months, and has been a year in this one, it's a reasonable bet a move is in the offing. Conversely some of the best developmental managers you can work for have been in the same assignment for many years. They have patience, have worked with many junior people, and even may have a reputation in the organization for bringing along future superstars. Finding one of these people may change your whole offer-evaluation process.

It's expecting a lot for you to be able to pass judgement on all these factors once an offer is made. Don't try to do it alone. One of the purposes of developing a contact network of professionals is so you can go back to them for an opinion. Should you sell aluminum siding on a straight commission basis? How does a life insurance training program work, especially when the support salary system begins to decrease monthly? What do you think about this company? Have you ever had any dealings with it?

That very question was asked by an applicant to a professional contact who in turn talked to some of his associates. The contact came up with a very shaky opinion of the outfit in question. The offer appeared to be a good one with a substantial starting salary and the promise of a gradual phase into the business. It also

> *If the choice is between going to work and not going to work, you place yourself in a less than advantageous position. Do everything you can to keep from boxing yourself in.*

happened to be the only offer being considered. The applicant wanted to look at the positive side, so when a title and office were added to the package, it looked (and was) too good to be true. After three weeks on the job with minimal training and support, he found he was expected to begin producing all kinds of results. He was matched up with another recent hire and put into a highly competitive environment. He responded as best he could, and actually learned a great deal during his year in the trenches, but departed shortly after his twelfth month to find a somewhat more ethical opportunity. His competitive peer left soon after, when a large commission was somehow computed down to about 10 percent of what the compensation plan prescribed.

These things happen and it is very difficult to make careful judgements, especially if you are looking at one offer at a time. If the choice is between going to work and not going to work, you place yourself in a less than advantageous position. At least go in with your eyes open, if that's the path you choose.

Do everything you can to keep from boxing yourself in. Getting multiple offers to come together all at the same time may seem like an unrealistic goal, but it's not impossible and definitely worth all the effort when you think about the options they create.

Whether it's winter holiday time in your junior year, or you have just graduated, don't let time pressure (or lack of time pressure) change your strategy. The discipline you must master is not to jump at the first opportunity once graduation nears or when you find yourself job hunting full time.

One final point. When you do accept an offer, it's a good idea to put together a letter to your complete contact network. You can wait until you are actually working if you would like, so that your announcement goes out on a letterhead. The important thing is that you keep everyone plugged in on the final result. You may be tempted to do a form letter on someone's word processor; don't let the task of doing ten or twenty personal letters of announcement keep you from spreading the good news in good form to key players in your campaign.

Being able to say that you looked over several bona fide offers and went with your first choice is the best possible ending to your opening move into the job market.

CHAPTER 12

GRAD SCHOOL,

THE LAW,

MBA'S:

TAKING

COURSES

> **It is not a bad idea to take a quick look at total life span to see, if by the time you get all the credentials, there will be sufficient time left to do much else.**

There is body of thought that says that people are in school far too long. If you are a college junior or senior and have spent the majority of your life on earth as a student, you may tend to agree with this point of view.

On the other hand, if brain surgery is going to be your thing, or if you have your heart set on designing buildings, or even becoming a Jesuit, you have many, many more years of school ahead of you.

The list of things that you can do without additional school far exceeds those positions and careers that require more academic credentials. The problem arises when the credentials are optional or may not be needed.

It is not a bad idea to take a quick look at total life span to see, if by the time you get all the credentials, there will be sufficient time left to do much else.

YOU ARE HIGHLY MARKETABLE AS IS

One career that has been popular for many years has been that of professional student. Getting sponsorship for this occupation has never been easy, but those who decide that this is the way to go somehow always seem to manage. Eventually, they legitimize their choice by doing some kind of teaching or research work and so become members of the academic community by either gradual design or default. There are worse ways to go through life than with leather-patched elbows or briefcases full of blue books. Almost everyone has the option of never leaving school.

In moving from the known to the unknown, there is always a certain comfort in the devil you know versus the devil you don't know.

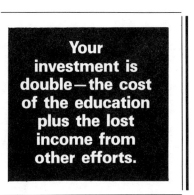

Your investment is double—the cost of the education plus the lost income from other efforts.

In moving from the known to the unknown, there is always a certain comfort in the devil you know versus the devil you don't know. Many people who enjoy a degree of success in academics find it difficult to leave. Getting good grades and going to lectures, labs, and seminars can be habit forming. There is the social camaraderie of student life, plus the structure and time-frame that create patterns to one's existence.

Bear one fact in mind as you begin thinking about "going on." In spite of grad school application and acceptance procedures, in reality, you are purchasing an educational service from which you hope to get some benefit. At the same time you are purchasing this service, you are investing your time and effort to the exclusion of most other activity. Your investment is double—the cost of the education plus the lost income from other efforts.

Just the terminology of "taking" courses, when in fact they are being purchased, or of "going" to grad school, when you are investing in graduate school in both fees and lost income, tends to fuel the delusion of a student life without end. Becoming learned is one thing. Adopting the economics of the learned life-style is another.

If your graduate pursuit tends to be vocational and optional, as is the case for example with an MBA, double alarm bells should ring. If law school has appeal because it will fit nicely into several as yet undetermined career paths, it might be wise to see if you can find a horse to put in front of the cart, before you buy one very expensive cart.

> **If your graduate pursuit tends to be vocational and optional, as is the case with an MBA, double alarm bells should ring.**

> **Be advised that male or female, biology or rhetoric major, you are marketable as is. There is no need to add anything.**

It could well be that you have made the mental break with college, and can't wait to get going at the earliest possible date. Even with those so inclined, there is a latent desire to join a training program, get some additional background, pick up more marketable skills.

Each year a nationally known secretarial school sells a course designed for college graduates, mostly to women, so that they can acquire "marketable skills." Be advised that male or female, biology or rhetoric major, you are marketable as is. There is no need to add anything. In fact, you probably have been marketable for several years and didn't know it. Those who have had to interrupt their studies for one reason or another often have done very well in the marketplace, so degrees, while desirable, are not life-dependent elements.

What makes a person marketable is often just the having of marketing skills and applying them to the task of selling oneself. Marketing skills, as we have seen by this time, are not terribly complex. They are more a matter of contact and follow up, questions and personal chemistry.

"Picking up" an economics course and some computer science may seem to be logical steps in making an entry into business from a liberal arts education; in fact, basic business economics can be understood in fifteen minutes and the biggest computer problem you will face may well be the operation of your office telephone and mastering the techniques of transferring calls. The regular reading of the *Wall Street Journal,* will bring you a formidable business education in only a few months.

Business schools, staffed with Ph.Ds in business (which usually precludes any actual business experience) are like zoos populated with stuffed animals. They just aren't real.

TO MBA OR NOT TO MBA

Business schools, staffed with Ph.Ds in business, (which usually precludes any actual business experience) are like zoos populated with stuffed animals. They just aren't real.

Case studies may have realistic rings to them with recognizable company names and products, but business does not operate on the case method, even though many business schools do. Seldom are business people required to analyze quantitative data and develop a detailed solution for a clear-cut problem. One of the best strategies is to ignore as many problems as possible, while seeking out areas of strength upon which to build results. The human dynamic of that process cannot be simulated in case studies.

Specialization is another "excuse" for remaining a student. You want to become an expert, concentrating on a specialized area to make yourself more marketable. Even an average depth of specialization, however, cannot be achieved in the most advanced courses. This occurs naturally in a relatively short period of time right on the job. When you concentrate on one aspect of a process day-in and day-out for weeks and months on end, you can get very, very good at that aspect, and in fact, become an authority very quickly. Specialization is best acquired in the doing. The result is technically more sound, plus you are being paid and making career progress at the same time.

> **Specialization is best acquired in the doing. The result is technically more sound, plus you are being paid and making career progress at the same time.**

> **The idea that you can't make it in business without an MBA is an idea the the business schools have sold, not the businesses.**

The challenge at this point is to make a realistic evaluation of the options open to you. Be careful not to buy additional schooling, when it may not be either necessary, useful, or ultimately profitable. The idea that you can't make it in business without an MBA is an idea that the business schools have sold, not the businesses.

Women especially, but men, too, are told that to be competitive in the tough world of business an MBA is essential. This is very comfortable advice. School is for the most part a relatively noncompetitive environment. It's comfortable to get the grades, and be in a familiar environment.

The world of work, on the other hand, is highly competitive; it is not as comfortable nor is it a known entity. Unfortunately credentials and degrees do not change the situation. Getting involved in the day-to-day action is what builds the skills necessary to survive and prosper. Postponing that involvement just provides a costly delay without the promised advantages. If you still want to go to grad school just because it appeals to you, go ahead. It can't do you much harm, and it offers a warm and comfortable, if sometimes harried, life.

One major company supposedly required an advanced degree from one of a half dozen choice schools as criteria for entry into its marketing department. A quick survey of the people working in the department revealed that only one or two of the employees had these credentials. The criteria were used just to screen out applicants. Those who actually had the degrees requested were interviewed, but usually were told that no entry-level positions were available.

How would you like to have spent twenty-or forty-thousand dollars, two years of your life, and have forfeited many more thousands of dollars in income just to get caught in that little Catch-22 screening gimmick? In fact, the company hired anyone it thought would fit in

The best way to learn is most often to do, not to study. There is a paradox in specialized degree programs that is difficult to overcome. If the real thing is available, what benefit is an academic simulation?

its marketing operation, but the supply was so great for this highly visible outfit that some kind of inside contact usually was required. Everyone else was just told that the advanced degree was needed. It saved the marketing managers a lot of time.

Things are not always as they seem. An excellent investment of time and effort is to go and check it out for yourself. Actually going to work for an organization will teach you a great deal in a very short period of time. The best way to learn is most often to do, not to study.

There is a paradox in specialized degree programs that is difficult to overcome. If the real thing is available, what benefit is an academic simulation?

One junior manager decided that he would never amount to anything in his big Fortune 500 company without an MBA. He asked the training manager for advice. He was told that the only major value of the degree in that company was social. He decided to enroll in an evening school, locally, for the degree, unaware that socially, night school didn't count.

Several months later the training director dropped by the new manager's office to say hello. Our manager was hard at work on a simulated new product launch project for his class. Believe it or not, sitting on his work-table, pushed to one side for his classwork, was a real multi-million dollar product introductory program which was a part of his everyday job.

Both the real and the simulated project eventually were launched and completed. A 15 percent share of market was achieved by the real product, and a B was earned by the class project. The junior manager never realized that his real job was teaching him far more technically than any of the courses he was paying to attend.

In several years, our manager's graduation picture hung proudly behind his desk. Later, he was transferred to a division that was eventually dissolved. He never made the anticipated climb up the ladder for which he had so long prepared. His preparation in reality bore little relationship to what was required. He misread the career requirements in his company by spending several years to join the wrong club.

Club membership and status can be invaluable in some situations, but try not to confuse that value with the content and intent of advanced degree programs. And, of course, pick the right club to start with.

> **To be an informed buyer of advanced degrees and additional schooling requires a good deal of consumer research.**

THE CHALLENGE
OF SELF-EDUCATION

It is an excellent idea to go to work in a field and survey the career results of others with and without advanced degrees.

After gaining some in-the-field background, try going back to school to survey a few courses for relevancy of content. Just audit a course or two, or ask if you can sit in for a couple of sessions. Look over the text and a syllabus. It won't be difficult to make an informed value judgement.

Many courses are offered on subjects that actually can't be taught. These subject areas can be learned, but only over extended time periods of actual experience. It is difficult to know this without the perspective gained as a result of actually doing some of these jobs in the field. Supervisory management is taught in one semester or even in three-day seminars. Unfortunately for those investing in these programs, to begin to learn how to be a supervisor takes eighteen to twenty-four months of field work alongside an experienced supervisor. Assistant managers' jobs are designed to create just this experiential learning situation. To be an informed buyer of advanced degrees and additional schooling requires a good deal of consumer research.

Graduate school is often thought of as a place to go, if you don't know what you want to do. It can be, but it is a very expensive place to visit, and sooner or later, the same starting decision must be made.

Long-term career choices are best made in the field after seeing and testing many options. The sooner you get face to face with reality, the sooner you will be able to see advanced degrees in the light of their projected benefits. Reading some autobiographies will give you an idea of how others have handled choices, either for better or worse. Your task is not to see the future, but rather not to put blind faith in the present as a means of achieving some vague future goal.

Once you have a basic degree, the challenge of self-education begins. With even a cursory reading program, you can develop not only wide interests, but in-depth knowledge of almost any discipline. There are popularly written books on almost any topic with bibliographies leading to a whole series of follow-up publications.

Education doesn't stop when you graduate; it starts. Selecting your own material in view of your own developing needs is a new freedom in learning acquired when you leave campus. It's not necessary to have someone else develop your curriculum. You can do it yourself with great variety and benefit.

One of the advantages of self-education is that it can be highly directed. You can focus on specifics that may be given only passing reference in some course, but are especially meaningful to you.

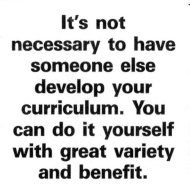

It's not necessary to have someone else develop your curriculum. You can do it yourself with great variety and benefit.

> **Degrees are not the keys to the future. They do not unlock doors.**

THE PAUSE PHILOSOPHY

These are all good reasons to challenge the standard progression from undergraduate to graduate education. The pause philosophy says there should be a break between these two phases of formal education. That's an excellent option to exercise because the more outside experience you can build, the more informed your decision will be as to whether, when, and where to go for further formal education. Some business schools set this pause as a requirement for admission. However, they recommend a two-year pause where four to five years is more appropriate.

Following in the beaten path has to be questioned. Making assumptions about the value of advanced degrees can be costly.

Many schools publish salary figures for their graduates. Be careful of these numbers, if for no other reason than the source. These schools are businesses themselves and must fill seats to survive. Therefore, salary levels may be inflated. A graduate's success in a field cannot necessarily be measured by a specific educational experience. Causal relationship has never been established. The return on investment may look good, but may not be born out by the facts.

Degrees are not the keys to the future. They do not unlock doors. They are expensive, time-consuming, and should be questioned, especially if there is no intervening period between undergraduate and graduate work.

If you are so dedicated and directed that you know exactly what you want, and law school or medical school is an absolute requirement, then go to it. You are the one that the system is designed for. Let's hope your decision is correct and your investment pays off.

If there are options, ask as many questions as you can. Think in terms of breaking away from the college environment just for the experience that can be gained by doing so. You will be able to come back, at almost anytime. It's not difficult to get back into the academic swing of things, if ultimately that is where you want to be. Your re-entry will, in fact, be much more beneficial as a result of gaining the additional outside perspective.

It may well be true that the longer you can put off an advanced degree, the more valuable it will be, if and when you decide to go for it. So, too, the longer you put off an advanced degree, the less you may find you need one.

Don't rush this one. Try generating some income before you make additional plans to dispose of it.

CHAPTER 13

STARTING YOUR OWN BUSINESS

You can take a course on downhill ski racing, but there is no way to address the experience of going fifty plus miles per hour down the side of an icy mountain.

Going out on your own directly out of college is not impossible and, in fact, with the right combination of circumstances it may just be a great time in your life to give it a shot.

Taking a course on being an entrepreneur might raise your level of excitement and interest, but that is only a pale description of some of the mechanics of the process. Reality in this case must be lived to be appreciated. You can take a course on downhill ski racing, but there is no way to address the experience of going fifty plus miles per hour down the side of an icy mountain. You can watch films, talk to those who have done it, and read endless books on the subject. None of this will bring you close to the actual situation. The book on how to make love tells you first to get a partner. Your own business, downhill ski racing, and love-making are not best handled in print.

There are all kinds of profiles describing the characteristics of people who start their own businesses. Don't worry about those because the exceptions are the rule in doing it yourself.

DON'T SET OUT TO
CHANGE THE WORLD. . . . .YET

There is only one key element in starting a business and that is that you must find a customer who will pay you for what you do or produce. Once you have a customer, or numbers of customers, everything else can be made to work out one way or another.

Although it is very appealing and romantic to be innovative and creative, spending your energies on developing something totally new, think in terms of doing something for somebody who will pay you for it, because you do it better than it has ever been done before.

The degree of difficulty in gaining customers is grossly underrated by most people starting out. Assuming that something will sell is the assumption that kills more companies quicker than any other. If you must create both a company and a market at the same time, the degree of difficulty rises geometrically. Entering an existing market reduces start-up time, funding needs, and risk. As with everything else in the arena, there are exceptions. Think in terms of improving odds, rather than going for long shots.

If you want to start your own business directly out of school, you have the advantage of low overhead (especially if you can move in with parents or friends), high energy, enthusiasm, and a fair amount of blissful ignorance of what "can't" be done. On the other side of the ledger, experience and a track record are lacking, resources are minimal, and contacts are in short supply. With that kind of a line-up, you will find that any start-up will be difficult.

The degree of difficulty in gaining customers is grossly underrated by most people starting out.

If you must create both a company and a market at the same time, the degree of difficulty rises geometrically.

> **An ice cream shop that delivers specialty items is more within the range of a recent graduate than an electric car company.**

Becoming innovative in small ways in a small-scale standard-type enterprise is probably more realistic than setting out to change the world. An ice cream shop that delivers specialty items is more within the range of a recent graduate than an electric car company, for example. If you have an idea for an electric car, don't be discouraged; just be prepared to support yourself while you attempt to get your idea into action.

Ideally, you get a customer to provide funds by selling your service or product to them. Those funds plus your own sweat equity produce additional product or services allowing you to operate without outside funding. If you can continue that cycle, you will have solved the problem of overexposure and underfunding that stops most people before they begin.

Be careful not to think of the material things surrounding a business as an integral part of the business. An office, a computer, a brochure, stationery, business cards may seem to be necessities, but often you can avoid these costs. Customers and cash coming in are the only essentials.

Frederick Smith was a person of some means when he determined that the air freight business was set up all wrong. He believed that a single hub city, Memphis, Tennessee, and a fleet of dedicated jet aircraft could provide overnight package delivery across the country. He needed millions in capital before he could deliver his first package. The complete system had to be in place before he could begin. He then had to be able to entice customers who had never used this type of service before, because it hadn't existed. Federal Express is now history. It has one thing in common with most new ventures and that is that its creator had no idea how difficult it would be or how long it would take to make it work.

Most people run out of time and money long before they make it into the pages of business magazines. It's not that they don't have good ideas; it's just that the degree of difficulty is well beyond their means, especially right out of college. A proven sure thing is the objective.

> **Most people run out of time and money long before they make it into the pages of business magazines.**

WORKING YOUR WAY INTO IT

One strategy, often adopted by people directly out of school who want to start their own businesses, is to set that as a goal while working for someone else. This provides the opportunity to gain knowledge, experience, contacts, and perhaps funding for the accomplishment of their entrepreneurial goal. This is ethical and realistic, and is done by many people. It solves the ignorance problem and keeps one alive and well, while still going for it.

The danger in this approach is that you will absorb too much knowledge, discover the real degrees of difficulty, and develop a comfort level and life-style that will slowly take you out of the race before you get in. On the flipside, the constraints of working within a structured organization or for someone whose competence may be in question, may provide the level of frustration necessary to get you out on your own.

On occasion, people start their own businesses while still in school and sometimes just expand efforts upon graduation. Campus-based businesses are often tied into a student market, but not always. The problem arises in being able to generate enough income to sustain the business after leaving college life.

Doing what you know is far more important than being innovative or creative.

If you have been in a business in a small way and know how it works, it's just possible that you will be able to scale it up slightly and make it work on a full-time basis. Running spring-break tours in exchange for your own free tickets can convert to the travel agency business with a little luck, timing, and hard work. Doing what you know is far more important than being innovative or creative. Creativity, while exciting, just increases the risk factor, at a time when additional risk is not what is needed.

Having the ability to convince others of the merits of your product or service is most important of all. The communication skills that play such a big part in general career exploration are even more important if you intend starting something on your own. Operating without a boss, structure, and organization or any of the things associated with a conventional job is all well and good, but you are responsible to the marketplace, customers, suppliers, bankers or backers, and a whole host of support people who may not work directly for you but must somehow perform in order for you to be able to run your business. Getting what you want done through this maze of people requires a talent for being able to attract and mobilize people to your side. If you have this skill by reason of your being able to get organizations and activities to function for you, that could be an added plus on the go side of the page.

> # One distinct advantage of a low-risk, low-profile start-up is that if it fails, you will somehow survive and will be able to find an organizational home with no more difficulty than if you hadn't tried it in the first place.

A LOW RISK START-UP

One distinct advantage of a low-risk, low-profile start-up is that if it fails, you will somehow survive and will be able to find an organizational home with no more difficulty than if you hadn't tried it in the first place. Approaching an organization after a year on your own, even with a business failure, is not all bad. It reinforces the wisdom of those company people who are interviewing you in their own choice of safety and security. It's the "I told you so" factor.

You also have the option of trying again. One strike doesn't mean you are out. The degree of financial loss incurred is important, as there must be a point beyond which it will not be prudent to go. Committing every financial resource you have down to the last nickel looks good in the success story write-up, but keeping an untouchable reserve for getting going again if things don't work out is a wiser, if less glamorous, strategy.

> **When things go well, a partner is great for sharing the effort and the glory. When things do not go well, the sharing of serious problems is not as much fun.**

PARTNERSHIPS AND OTHER LEGALITIES

Because being on your own is risky, lonely, and exhausting, a partner could be the answer to your prayers. Someone equally committed with complementary talents has often made the difference.

If that is the formula, why don't eight or ten little partnerships rocket into the Fortune 500 each year? Why only one, or none? A reading of the history of any successful start-up shows that there were all kinds of forces at work besides the fortunate or sometimes rocky partner relationship.

When things go well, a partner is great for sharing the effort and the glory. When things do not go well, the sharing of serious problems is not as much fun.

Degrees of commitment vary. Most people involved with partnership agreements will tell you that a vital factor is the out-clause, because it almost invariably is exercised for better or for worse. Who brings what to the party is again an added factor in the already complex equation of a new venture. Most success stories mention the time when one partner dropped out or was bought out; that should tell you something about avoiding this kind of difficulty in advance, if at all possible.

While on the subject of legal structures of business, the cost of incorporation is often not necessary for a start-up. Don't worry about the details of incorporation until large amounts of cash are getting in the way, and then things can be worked out. All that is necessary to start a business legally is an internal revenue number which allows you to operate as a proprietorship. One federal form will get it for you, and that is so the government's share of your enterprise finds its way into the U.S. Treasury. If you can keep it as simple as a proprietorship, that's just less you must worry about.

VENTURE CAPITAL

Generation of cash seems to be something that decides the go, no-go factor at all stages.

What about venture capital? If you have a good idea, shouldn't you be able to make the rounds of venture capitalists, and convince one to buy in? This is always a possibility, but the venture people operate under some rules of business which they have found to be best for them. First, the business must be high growth and at a predetermined point must be saleable in order to allow the venture capitalists to get a return on their investment.

Rapid high growth is measured against other companies that have been down the same road. Innovative high technology firms are the current measuring sticks and they have established high standards against which your idea and business must compare favorably.

One of the means of comparison will be a business plan. This highly structured booklet is a combination sales forecast, budget, wish list and financial dream document that must convince people used to reading these things that you and your idea are something special. Venture capitalists earn their living by trying to go only with the winners. The degree of success necessary to make an idea a good investment for a venture capitalist is in the hundreds of millions of dollars.

They also look for a team with a track record in making things happen. Getting the yearbook out isn't something that will carry a lot of weight with that group, unless you possess an inordinate amount of skill to make that yearbook project come off sounding like the Manhattan Project. If you are that good, you proably don't need the venture capital people in the first place.

So it's not as if there is a big Catch-22, but doing your own thing is a difficult challenge at any time, and for new college graduates it's a task that few attempt and that fewer are able to carry off.

In talking with successful entrepreneurs—not necessarily ones directly out of school, but just highly successful practitioners—it seems that over and above genius and other similar characteristics, there seems to be a good deal of luck involved.

They met and impressed the right person. They did the right thing for the wrong reasons. They were at a particular place or in a particular industry as it began to move. You can go for all this just the way they did, but you might as well have surveyed the territory and reviewed how others have done it or at least what some of the rules appear to be. Taking some of the rules and knowingly disregarding them is also a posssbility, but this increases risk factors at a time when it usually is not a good idea to do so.

One common problem will be that everyone, including this author, will tell you how difficult it is to start your own business. Somehow you must overcome all of this negative opinion. You must press on in the face of what appears certain failure to others. Of course, if it becomes actual failure, you have merely tested reality and are free to lick your wounds, and try something else. There is little or no stigma attached to an unsuccessful end. In

> **There is little or no stigma attached to an unsuccessful end. In fact, you are often admired just for the attempt. It shows you are made of special stuff.**

fact, you are often admired just for the attempt. It shows you are made of special stuff. That doesn't ease much of the pain when things come apart, but it's one less thing to worry about as the ship sinks.

There is a balance to look for. How can I get this thing going without a financial disaster? Can I get up and running and survive for a while? Can I take the time I bought and turn that into results that will buy a little more time? If you can create a little success, there is always the chance you can parlay that into a little something more. What will it take to live through the down periods? When they come, there is no way of knowing how long they will last or if, in fact, they will turn around at all.

Strength of character is not usually listed as a requirement, but you can bet that it must be in there if you want to give your own thing a try.

Getting a solid return on what you do is important because a little success must sometimes be stretched over the period of time necessary to generate more return. High margins allow you to live on low volume. If you can eventually build both high margins and high volume, you are off and running.

If someone is already getting high margins and you can get yourself started slightly below the market, you will have a chance to become the "economy" source. You also can try going in above the market, selling the concept that you are the best there is. That is another way of saying that you are the highest priced. If you have the quality of goods and service, again, you may make it work.

The variations are almost infinite. There are so many rules, there are almost no rules. In retrospect, everything becomes clear. The success books fill the shelves; book writers don't do chapters on those who don't make it. Not to end on a negative note, but those are the stories that would be best to read if only they were written. Running in a race and building your own track to run on at the same time are not for everyone.

Best wishes and good luck, if this is the chapter of the book that becomes most meaningful to you.

Running in a race and building your own track to run on at the same time are not for everyone.

CHANGE
IS CONSTANT;
PLAN
ACCORDINGLY

The step-by-step pyramid builder misses something along the way.

S etting goals and making plans have proven to be one of the most effective ways of achieving results. Too many people let life carry them along and then at some point find themselves dissatisfied with the results or current circumstances. There are also those who operate from constantly up-dated five-year plans leading to broad objectives many years in the future.

It's hard to know which side of the balance carries more liability. Letting life run you or picking off targets of opportunity can't be the best way to go, but the step-by-step pyramid builder misses something along the way as well.

The mid-ground seems to offer all the benefits of achieving objectives without the rigidity of total single-mindedness.

AMIDST A FAST-MOVING WORLD

Change and flexibility in careers are definitely the rule rather than the exception. They are not only normal and healthy, but they add variety, and in some cases, force adaptations that lead to unanticipated benefits in life-style. Mobility is good. Controlling it is better. Controlled or uncontrolled, it is a fact of life you must accept. A flexible strategy is probably the most productive start-up approach, which will serve you over the long term as well.

One way you can test out this view is to go to the alumni office and see if it does "where-are-they-now" type books for anniversary classes. Usually for a twenty-fifth or fiftieth class reunion, members of the class are asked to write up a little piece on what they have been doing since graduation. The nature of this type of project tends to draw only successful class members to contribute. That's all right because you are not conducting a scientific study, but rather just trying to get a feel for the paths that have been taken. If this material is available, try reading large amounts of it. These mini-autobiographies will turn up some unusual patterns. Sometimes the geography covered is hard to believe, but this is real life.

If your alumni office doesn't do this kind of thing, call other colleges for this same kind of material. The twists and turns are the elements most common. There will be some linear career stories in these surveys because as noted, single-mindedness does achieve results. At various points, you too will have to become single-minded in order to do what you want. By far, the most common patterns indicate changing values and life-styles which require much more adjustment than anticipated when you are at the beginning and trying to make entry decisions.

> *Mobility is good. Controlling it is better.*

> **It's better to give different things a chance than to follow a rigid plan, only to discover that it didn't provide all you anticipated.**

> **Mobility requires strength and confidence.**

Change and its concurrent adjustments can be very positive, so constantly looking for alternatives tends to produce a stream of opportunities. Some will be good and will lead in worthwhile directions; others will be blind alleys that will be difficult to escape. It's better to give different things a chance than to follow a rigid plan, only to discover that it didn't provide all you anticipated. A job is not forever, even though you must approach it that way for interview purposes. If something isn't working it may not be easy to walk away from it, but it will be far better than trying to force a situation or fit yourself into a mold that was never made for you. Mobility requires strength and confidence.

Because change is constant, we sometimes don't notice the subtle nature of the shifts in our environment. If you can chat with a parent or two, ask them to talk in detail about their lives and values when they were your age. See if you can draw out what day-to-day life was all about. See if you can get them to contrast their lives at that time with the memories they might have of their parents. It's a little frightening how few generations you have to probe to get back to travel by horse and buggy. Going the same distance into the future will give you an idea of the dramatic environmental change that may occur during the span of your career path.

What all this indicates is that having career plans with flexibility for many variables is best because change will always be with us. Accept it now.

> *Your transition from college to the outside world is a pretty dramatic change, but it is only the first of many. You are not looking for your life's work. You are just taking the first of many career steps.*

> *Organizations unrealistically try to hire people for life. People equally unrealistically look at opportunities with lifetime-type stars in their eyes.*

CHANGE IN YOUR PERSONAL WORLD

The forces causing individual career changes are all around us. A new boss with incompatible personal chemistry will sometimes mean a new organization for you. A division or company is either bought or sold and you may well find yourself on the surplus end. Room must be made for a family member in a business and you are either the room to be made, or the place you were going all of a sudden becomes filled by the heir apparent.

On the positive side, a new venture is being started by friends and you are asked to join in. Or you have an idea and decide to make the break. Family situations change and new horizons open as children graduate from college or head out on their own. All of these near and far eventualities are realities, and if you understand this as you set strategies and make plans, you will be able to focus on more workable options.

Your transition from college to the outside world is a pretty dramatic change, but it is only the first of many. You are not looking for your life's work. You are just taking the first of many career steps. Viewing yourself as being self-employed even while working for an organization is a perspective that you should keep constantly in mind. You are actually selling your services to your employer in return for monetary consideration and benefits. Becoming overly dependent on one business concern is not in your best interests. Making a particular job "your whole life" can be very satisfying, but it also can be very dangerous. Building a highly specialized background may require a little backtracking if the demand for that specialty is reduced.

One engineer with a strong grounding in physics worked in the aerospace field on one phase of earth atmosphere re-entry research. After years of effort, all of the basic problems were solved and the program wound down. He had climbed to the top of this field. The field itself suddenly no longer existed. He had to climb back down, generalizing his skills by moving from one company to another for a few years. He shifted from engineering to general management and from aerospace to industrial goods. The shift took several years and was not easy, but he is glad in retrospect he had the chance to move his career in its new direction. Career obsolescence is a new reality in these fast-paced times.

Planned mobility at the early stages of a career will serve you well later on. This way change will be easier to handle. Organizations unrealistically try to hire people for life. People equally unrealistically look at opportunities with lifetime-type stars in their eyes. Statistics tell a far different story. Assignments last less than two years and even if you stay in one organization for a greater period of time, the dynamics of the situation change around you, so nothing is really static.

When you do move from one situation to another, from company to company, you go through a slate-cleaning process which erases all past errors and magnifies all past positive accomplishments. Starting fresh every so often, at a little higher level, is one of the best ways to achieve a promotion and advancement. It takes considerable courage to pursue this route, but at least you are in control.

Riding with a dying industry or company can be debilitating while you are there, and can also put a cloud on future moves by having been associated with a less than successful venture. These things can be turned around, but sometimes it's very difficult. After an involuntary separation from one company, one manager spent almost a year looking for a suitable opportunity. He eventually had to drop the "suitable" part and just get himself inside and working. He took on a challenge with a small, troubled manufacturer and within a few months found himself putting out fires and trying to keep things going. Chapter 11 followed and he had to then learn to operate under the bankruptcy laws. He spent almost a year in very turbulent times. The company could not be reorganized or sold, and it eventually folded with its minimal assets being sold to satisfy creditors. In the process, one of the prospective buyers recognized the talent of the manager and hired him to run a new start-up operation as soon as the lights went out at the dying company.

Having the skill and resilience to ride through those kinds of career ups and downs must be acquired. If you can hang on long enough, there seems to be some kind of a happy or semi-happy ending for almost everyone. The time it takes to arrive there is an unknown, but the adaptability of people is just about unlimited. Realizing this tends to accelerate the process.

> *Riding with a dying industry or company can be debilitating while you are there, and can also put a cloud on future moves.*

> *The open mind-set is important from the beginning. Nothing is forever. Plan accordingly.*

THE OPEN
INDEPENDENT MIND

The open mind-set is important from the beginning. Nothing is forever. Plan accordingly. Building reasonable cash resources is easier to do at the time of an income increase, than when expenses are growing and a situation is deteriorating. Developing a wide circle of professional associates and maintaining that circle with regular contact will add to your independence. Going strong for the big opportunity is easier to do with perspective built over several different assignments, and with a backup Plan B and reasonable time schedule.

Dual careers add up to substantial incomes; using one career to leverage time to make a solid move in the other is a wise employment of your assets. Shifting dominance in dual careers is something couples continue to struggle with. One student entered the insurance field while his wife taught part-time at a private school. In mid-life his career opportunities flattened out, while she went on to become head of a prestigious private school. Their relocations shifted to follow her career, with his career becoming the backup as he went into development work for non-profit organizations. How can you plan for that kind of career path? The answer is that you can't, but again flexibility rather than long-term single-mindedness often provides the overall best results.

It used to be that parents advised their daughters to learn to type or go into nursing or whatever, so that they would have "something to fall back on." That now becomes good advice for both sons and daughters, and in a much broader sense. Basic and general skills in writing, speaking, questioning, and listening are the new fall-back skills in an age of overspecialization, rapid obsolescence, and emerging technology.

Constantly working on general, transferable skill development and a broad-based contact network are ways of assuring smooth transitions as new opportunities present themselves, and old ones fade out.

Accept the fact that almost everyone gets fired once or twice in a lifetime and that these are just unplanned versus planned transition points. They usually happen to be highly traumatic, but once the bleeding slows all the same rules of change apply. One of the best ways to avoid being fired is to be a step ahead in the mobility game. Reading change signals early and not becoming emotionally attached to what you may perceive as security are some of the challenges of change. An inside third party who can tell you about how well you are getting along with your boss or about the health of the enterprise is of obvious value. It is just about impossible to win a shootout when you don't have a gun. Being fast on your career feet is the only sure winning option.

One very talented executive built his career in small high-growth companies. He developed almost a sixth sense when things began to take a turn for the worse. He was very fast on his feet. He has done very well for himself financially. He likes the excitement. He is good at his profession. Yet, his list of employers runs into double figures. His flexibility is extreme, but it does provide a graphic example of the idea.

It used to be that parents advised their daughters to learn to type or go into nursing or whatever, so that they would have "something to fall back on." That now becomes good advice for both sons and daughters, and in a much broader sense.

Being fast on your career feet is the only sure winning option.

Provided you have real as opposed to fast-track or exposure assignments, you can gain as much background and salable experience in twelve months as in eighteen or thirty-six months. Be very conservative in your decisions to wait out situations. Time in grade in one position is never totally wasted, but it could be put to far better use with a more rapid assessment and a subsequent move. Career mobility is an excellent antidote for stress disease. The fight or flight response to conflict has a third alternative; stay put and worry. This is probably the worst of all. The earlier you build the self-image and self-confidence to view yourself as a valued contributor the better. You will be a stronger independent supplier of labor and service once you accept that role.

> *The fight or flight response to conflict has a third alternative; stay put and worry. This is probably the worst of all.*

A BROADER VIEW OF YOUR JOB

Many careers offer in-and-out type paths that are seldom considered at entry. The opposite number of the purchasing agent is the sales representative. The advertising account executive must deal with a product manager or marketing vice-president. The consultant works with the company president.

All of those types of relationships are switchable. It is possible to learn enough on one side of the desk to make the move to the other side. You can uncover some

> **It is possible to learn enough on one side of the desk to make the move to the other side.**

interesting career paths by turning the "what do you want to be?" question around and asking people "what did they want to be?" You will find major and early shifts are far more common than you might expect.

Looking for a no-travel or low-travel position during the years of bringing up children should not be discounted. If you set that as an objective, there are plenty of ways to make it work. For those who want to stay single there are "go everywhere, see everyplace" type careers where high mobility is valued. Sometimes all of this can be done within one organization.

One woman joined a major airline as a counter ticket agent, worked her way into management, and then accepted station assignments all over the United States, taking three weeks vacation in Hawaii each year for mental health recovery. She landed a facilities chief position in a three-hundred person telephone reservations installation and decided to stay put when she met and married someone from that area. The airline was smart enough to reclassify her as location stable. She and the airline have continued a productive relationship, now spanning almost twenty years. She still takes her Hawaiian winter break each year, only now she is escorted. In this case, the person managed high mobility and change satisfactorily within one large company. Sometimes it can be done.

The simple formulas of "a couple of years with a big company" or the "start-you-own-business or get-a-piece-of-a-smaller-company" just don't cover the variety available. One salesman worked as a direct representative for a company and then was offered a position with a manufacturers representatives' firm. Because the field was related, he asked his company if it would let him take his line with him on the new job. The company agreed and several years later when he went out on his own, the company transferred its agency representation again to let the same man continue to handle its business.

One man was fired by a major medical company and went to work for a smaller one. The boss who fired him was later hired by the same small company and subsequently fired him again. Several years later, the small company acquired another outfit and who turned up on its payroll, but the poor soul who was just trying to earn a living in his industry. He was phased out for the third time by the same executive who still had a low opinion of his abilities. There was no way to predict this twenty-year chain of events. The milkshake mixer salesman who buys a hamburger stand and creates the fast-food industry, the manager fired by National Cash Register (NCR) and subsequently names his new company International Business Machines (IBM) in order to go one up on his former employer—none of this can be planned. The success biographical literature is full of interesting

Look at some short-term goals and see if they are attainable, and also if you want to pay the price in effort.

> **It takes courage to upset your level of comfort. It's almost always easier to wait it out, at least for a while.**

turns of events in careers, markets, and destinies. Read them for the fascinating twists and turns, but don't try to formalize your life based on some grand plan. Grab on to the versatility and excitement that a positive attitude toward change can produce.

Although you may have to pay a price in time and effort up front in order to get a return, be careful of twenty- and thirty-year pyramids to less than sure payoffs. Instant returns and rags-to-riches stories are fortunately rare, so you needn't worry about having to make those decisions early on. For many who do become financially successful at an early point in their careers, that very success causes problems seldom anticipated. "Let me try some of those problems" is a common response. Perhaps you will have your chance at them, if you don't lock yourself into some extended long-term plan.

Get started somewhere and see what it is like. Sit down in six months and assess what you are doing. Look at some short-term goals and see if they are attainable, and also if you want to pay the price in effort. Look closely at those who are ahead of you by either months or years. Ask yourself if you would like to change places with them, right now; no dues paying, just take over as senior person, vice-president, or whatever, making the assumption that you could do the job.

If the answer is "no" for any reason, then it's time to plan an exit move. It takes courage to upset your level of comfort. It's almost always easier to wait it out, at least for a while. Things change very slowly. Invest your time wisely but also have the courage to stay in charge of where you are going. Change, both self-induced as well as imposed, makes a career exciting and potentially rewarding. Taking change as the constant and shaping all other moves accordingly will keep you loose enough to be able to cope, act, react, and hopefully shape your share of a future career.

The business of getting jobs just begins after college. You will have many, many chances to write your own future chapters of this book. Best wishes in beginning and building an exciting and rewarding career.

> *Taking change as the constant and shaping all other moves accordingly will keep you loose enough to be able to cope, act, react, and hopefully shape your share of a future career.*

WILLIAMSON PUBLISHING CO.

BOX 185, CHURCH HILL ROAD,
CHARLOTTE, VERMONT 05445

More Good Books from
![W] WILLIAMSON PUBLISHING

To order additional copies of Jack Falvey's **After College**, please enclose $9.95 per copy plus $2.00 shipping. Follow "To Order" instructions on the last page.

STUDY ABROAD
The Astute Student's Guide
by David Judkins

Learn here about the various kinds of study abroad opportunities—who the "major players" are, what the lesser-known, unusual programs offer, how to pick the right program for your budget, your personal needs, your academic goals. All programs and all students are not equal; creating the right match is essential.

304 pages, 6 × 9, charts
Quality paperback, $12.95

INTERNATIONAL CAREERS
An Insider's Guide
by David Win

If you long for a career that combines the excitement of foreign lifestyles and markets, the opportunity to explore your own potential, the promise of monetary and personal reward, then learn from David Win how to get off the stateside corporate ladder and into the newly emerging areas of international careers. Now's the time!

224 pages, 6 × 9, charts
Quality paperback, $10.95

PARENTING THROUGH THE COLLEGE YEARS
From Application Through Graduation
by Norman Giddan, Ph.D., and Sally Vallongo

Don't drop out when your kids go off to college! They may need you in a different capacity, but they need you just the same. Here's all about this amazing 4 years in the lives of parents and their almost-adult children. A lifesaver in many, many ways!

192 pages, 6 × 9
Quality paperback, $9.95

WHAT'S NEXT?
Career Strategies After 35
by Jack Falvey

Falvey explodes myths right and left and sets you on a straight course to a satisfying and successful mid-life career. Bring an open mind to his book and you'll be on your way. A liberating book to help us all get happily back into work.

192 pages, 6 × 9
Quality paperback, $9.95

BIKING THROUGH EUROPE
A Roadside Travel Guide with 17 Planned Cycle Tours
by Denis & Tina Jaffe

The Jaffe's experience and knowledge of cycling through Europe makes for a one-of-a-kind book with 17 fabulous routes for you to choose from plus wonderful field-tested recommendations for accommodations, side routes, restaurants, and shops. These cycle vacations are dreams come true!

304 pages, 6 × 9, detailed maps & routes
Quality paperback, $13.95

HOW TO IMPORT A EUROPEAN CAR
The Gray Market Guide
by Jean Dugay

Here's everything you need to know to purchase a car in Europe, drive it on your vacation, and ship it legally into the United States. You can save up to 25% on foreign car purchases—at the very least pay for your whole trip in savings! Names, address for reliable European dealers, best U.S. conversion centers, shippers. Covers DOT, EPA, customs, financing, bonding. Cost comparison for 200 models. Authoritative.

192 pages, 8½ × 11, illustrated, tables.
Quality paperback, $13.95

THE CAMPER'S COMPANION TO NORTHERN EUROPE
A Campground & Roadside Travel Guide

THE CAMPER'S COMPANION TO SOUTHERN EUROPE
A Campground & Roadside Travel Guide
by Dennis & Tina Jaffe

More than just campground directories, these travel guides share the best of each country off-the-beaten path. The Jaffes rate over 700 campgrounds covering all of Northern Europe in one volume, Southern and Eastern Europe and Northern Africa in the other volume. Country-by-country campgrounds.

300 pages, 6 × 9, maps, tables.
Quality paperback, $13.95